Praise for *Service Habits*

If you are a service professional, this could be the most important book you ever read. Jaquie Scammell, Australia's leading expert on customer service, breaks down what world-class service looks like – and, more importantly, the process to achieve it.

This book takes you through the 21 habits that will create a service mindset and make world-class service habitual for you, your team and your organisation.

Practical, accessible, engaging and profound, *Service Habits* is compulsory reading for anyone in the business of service. (And make no mistake, if you are in business, you're in the business of service.)

Peter Cook, bestselling author of Implement

The quality of being present to others as the foundational service habit is the very definition of leadership. Service habits may be good for business success and profitability, but they are perhaps more powerfully good for culture; something that goes way beyond annual performance metrics.

In this book and all her work, Jaquie infuses a quality of consciousness and respect to the art of business. *Service Habits* is a way to get the spirit of service deeply embedded in your culture. Absorbing the habits should feel as much at home on the frontline as it should in your leadership team.

Matt Church, Founder, Thought Leaders

T0274158

One of the most important legacies a leader can leave is a culture that supports its people and clients. This is often the main challenge facing organisations, particularly human service organisations, and one that leaders and boards grapple with constantly.

I met Jaquie when I was trying to make sense of organisational culture and customer service and how to build an enduring platform for change that was going to work for both our people and our clients. What was different about Jaquie's approach was her ability to make service culture clear and simple, and translate this for all people in the organisation. *Service Habits* talks clearly about the value of relationships in service culture and this alone makes it extremely insightful. It is so topical for today's businesses and will help you develop a strategy for service culture for the future.

Jennifer Lawrence, CEO, Brightwater Care Group

Service Habits has something for everyone. It shows how small, simple steps create habits that build long-lasting relationships that underpin what service is all about. Whether it's using people's names always, understanding your impact on others, building rapid rapport in conversations or making first impressions your superpower, Jaquie explains how these and other habits are the foundations of service. Through practical examples, Jaquie challenges us to reflect on how our values show up in our behaviours toward others and gives helpful steps to embed small changes so they become service habits. If you care about people and service, this is a book you will devour and then want to talk about with colleagues, leaders and friends.

Jane McAloon, Strategic and Corporate Advisory/
Non Executive Director

Easy to connect and relate to, practical with simple anecdotes, Jacquie's book weaves a seamless narrative which identifies that to give great service is a more integrated concept than we might think. *Service Habits* prompts us not only to think and understand ourselves first and foremost, before we can improve the customer service, but also to be more cognisant and present with our customers and the environment in which we operate. More than a service manuscript, *Service Habits* is a tonic for improving the interactions we have with everyone we engage with.

Mario Volpe – Commercial Manager, ALH Group

Service excellence brings a value position to life in a world that has moved from products to promises. Jaquie's book intelligently captures the essential steps to reflect on our service habits and to remain relevant. It also helps us feel a strong connection and meaning with our work and makes it more valuable for our clients.

Ephraim Patrick (Partner, Leading Global Consulting Firm)

2ND ED

SERVICE HABITS™

21 habits to transform
your service culture

JAQUIE SCAMMELL

First edition published in February 2020 by Major Street Publishing Pty Ltd.
This second edition published in February 2022.

PO Box 106, Highett, Vic. 3190
E: info@majorstreet.com.au W: majorstreet.com.au
M: +61 421 707 983

A catalogue record for this book is available from the National Library of Australia

Printed book: 978-1-922611-26-0
Ebook: 978-1-922611-27-7

Cover design by Yianni Kouros
Internal design by Production Works
Printed in Australia by Ovato, an Accredited ISO AS/NZS 14001:2004 Environmental Management System Printer.

10 9 8 7 6 5 4 3 2 1

Disclaimer: The material in this publication is in the nature of general comment only, and neither purports nor intends to be advice. Readers should not act on the basis of any matter in this publication without considering (and if appropriate taking) professional advice with due regard to their own particular circumstances. The author and publisher expressly disclaim all and any liability to any person, whether a purchaser of this publication or not, in respect of anything and the consequences of anything done or omitted to be done by any such person in reliance, whether whole or partial, upon the whole or any part of the contents of this publication.

Contents

PILLAR 3: ACT CONSCIOUSLY **141**

About the author

Jaquie Scammell makes customer service engaging and effort-less. Referred to as Australia's leading customer service expert, she helps businesses remember that great service is simple, and a service interaction is an opportunity to elevate the ordinary moments in a day.

Her work is underpinned by a strong foundation of mindfulness. A trained yoga, meditation and pranayama teacher, Jaquie has an approach with leaders that is easy, human and relatable, which ultimately retrains mindsets and habits in service interactions.

She is the founder of ServiceQ, a company that exists to create training programs and experiences to help businesses achieve their potential with conscious leaders, engaged employees and loyal customers. Jaquie and her team at ServiceQ have helped organisations from a variety of industries, such as healthcare, mining and resources, finance, retail and energy, as well as stadiums and sports organisations. The commonality among these businesses is they want to improve the connection between employee and customer, and it's *Service Habits* – and the associated Service Habits programs – that help them achieve customer intimacy and elevate their customer-service culture.

Over 20 years, Jaquie has worked with thousands of frontline employees and their leaders, in hundreds of public and private sector organisations. Her techniques and tools reveal a deep appreciation for the human side of business and have evolved from her experience of working in organisations such as

McDonald's, Wembley National Stadium Limited (UK) and Melbourne & Olympic Parks (for the Australian Open tennis grand slam tournament).

She lives in the CBD of Melbourne, Australia, with her partner Costa, and loves nothing more than escaping to the Mornington Peninsula for nature, family time and a nice glass of pinot noir.

Service Habits is Jaquie's second book published by Major Street Publishing. Her first book, *Creating a Customer Service Mindset*, was published in 2018 and featured regularly on the weekly Top 50 Australian Business Book lists for 2018. Now available under the new title of *Service Mindset*, it has been given a fresh new look as part of Jaquie's *Service* series.

Jaquie's purpose is to elevate the ordinary moments, so that together we can provide a more conscious service experience. That's what this book will help you do.

Introduction

'I have sales targets to meet and a job to do; the fluffy stuff about service can wait.'

'If my staff thought about what the person on the other end of the phone could be feeling, we might have half a chance of making the customer happy.'

'I get frustrated and often get caught in a process-driven cycle, rather than getting to the bottom of the solution for the customers. No wonder they get frustrated.'

'We're so driven by technology; we're under pressure to work to a deadline and meet a target. I don't have time for idle chitchat with people.'

'I've become so busy at work, with critical tasks to be done, that customer service is a mere fraction of my priorities in a day. Besides, can we really ever make them happy?'

These are things I hear from service professionals every day – frontline staff, employees, team leaders and leaders of leaders. Whether you're in finance, telecommunications, events, hospitality or transport, one of your biggest problems is the never-ending effort to keep people happy. The needs of colleagues and customers are like the weather – they can change at any moment.

We all want more connection, meaning and ease in our day-to-day lives. We want less effort and drama and fewer obstacles – not to mention less work! Employees want employers to serve them with excellent employee benefits and working conditions, opportunities for growth and development, and a workplace that's positive and supportive of their wellbeing. Customers want businesses to serve them with urgency, genuine care and basic common sense, and to provide solutions that help them achieve what they're looking for.

SERVICE TODAY

Once upon a time, service was easy. There was less pressure and fewer expectations to meet in order to provide what we'd call 'quality service'. Being responsive was simple and satisfying, both internally and externally to the organisation. In the 21st century, however, we've become so focused on systems and speed that we've forgotten service still is, and always will be, about building long-lasting relationships.

The current customer-service model is flawed. If we look deeper, it's easy to see why:

- The majority of businesses externalise customer service as a project or key focus area – looking at dashboards and algorithms to help implement and enforce customer service strategies, and labelling customer service as though it were separate to the rest of the relationships in the business.

- The majority of leaders prioritise financial results and process efficiencies over customer service, which reduces opportunities for less planned, more unpredictable human interactions and investing in relationships throughout a day.

- The majority of frontline employees are conditioned to follow the rules and procedures, allowing very little room for intuitive judgement in social interactions.

Today, good service is in danger of disappearing altogether behind a barrier of organisational protocols designed to achieve efficiency rather than strong, sustainable relationships and results. Yet two-thirds of the jobs created between now and 2030 will be reliant on soft skills. Much of the boring, repetitive work will be performed by technology, while humans undertake interpersonal and creative roles that require uniquely human skills, like customer service.

Good service was once about competitive pricing and quality products, but it's now about creating a connection that cuts through all the noise and nice-to-haves. We've evolved from transactional needs to relational needs, from providing commodities to finding commonalities with others.

Relationships are higher-order representations of a business, a leader and an individual – they have greater long-term impact than lower-order representations such as systems. They're a direct influence on:

· workplace culture

· productivity

· connections and networks

· identity and reputation

· self-esteem and confidence

· a sense of belonging and of value.

If you're in the business of service, then you're in the business of relationships.

SMALL STEPS

The biggest myth about improving service in today's world is that you need to make a large transformational effort to see a positive shift. This is simply not true. Over the past few years, I've been fortunate to work with some brilliant organisations led by some extraordinary CEOs, and to have developed long-term relationships with frontline leaders and teams who are achieving incredible results by strengthening their relationships with people.

I asked myself, 'What is it that these leaders have been taught, and what are they teaching their teams? What allows people in service to be extraordinary with people in an era of digital distraction, system-based thinking and noise?' What I found was that people who can establish an emotional connection with others are often focused on how they behave and understand the impact their behaviour has on their service performance. Businesses and service professionals that take small steps to enhance relationships experience the biggest positive results. I've seen this time and time again.

> **Take small steps to strengthen the relationships with people you serve.**

Professor B.J. Fogg, who founded the Stanford Persuasive Technology Lab and wrote the book *Tiny Habits*, has been studying how to change human behaviour for the past twenty years. He's learned there are only three things that change people's behaviour for the long term:

1. having an epiphany
2. changing their environment
3. taking baby steps.

In this book, I'm choosing to look at number three on this list – taking baby steps – as the way to change behaviour. Having an epiphany and changing the environment may seem like quicker solutions, but taking baby steps is the most reliable and practical way to approach behaviour change in the modern-day workplace. That is what this book will help you with.

This idea of taking baby steps towards continuous improvement has been known for centuries, by the way. In the mid–20th century, *kaizen* – the notion that small, continuous, positive changes can result in major improvements – became a management concept:

KAI	+	ZEN	=	KAIZEN
(change)		(good/better)		(continuous improvement)

WHY HABITS? WHY THIS BOOK?

One of the reasons people find it difficult to positively transform their service culture is that they aren't realistic about the time it takes to make ongoing positive changes. There's a minimum time period for installing a habit (as explained later in this introduction), and perhaps past efforts have not felt significant or grand enough to lead to such critical outcomes as employee and customer happiness – but the truth is that you simply haven't stuck at the habit long enough. Regardless of what has or has not worked in the past, however, service is everyone's responsibility, and it's through small steps over time – through small daily habits – that you'll improve the relationships that matter to you and the business.

So, what do I mean by small daily habits? And why do they work? Habits experts like B.J. Fogg and James Clear (speaker and author of *Atomic Habits*, who has taught more than 10,000 leaders, managers and coaches) explain that we are drawn to repeat behaviours that make us feel good. Once you repeat a behaviour many times, it eventually becomes automatic and a habit is formed.

In service, in work – in life, even – it's not what you do but how you do it that determines the impact you have on yourself and others. This book is about the *how* of service. It uncovers the habits at work that will limit your effectiveness in business and prevent you from becoming your best professional self. You'll learn how to sustain behaviours to form new and improved habits.

To create service habits that deepen your relationships with those you serve, you need to make continuous improvements in three areas – or 'pillars' – of service, which are discussed in detail in this book:

- *Pillar 1: Know yourself (habits 1 to 7).* Service starts with you. Before you can even consider the customer, you need an awareness of how you show up and how present you are.
- *Pillar 2: Understand others (habits 8 to 14).* Through the process of empathy, you are able to make people feel seen, heard and understood and create greater connections.
- *Pillar 3: Act consciously (habits 15 to 21).* Understand how your behaviours throughout ordinary moments impact someone's life, and know how to manage yourself when dealing with uncomfortable or unusual situations.

The service habits I'll explain will help you gain greater awareness of your own behaviour and a better understanding of others, so that you can manage yourself in a world full of ambiguity and change. As a result, you'll:

- feel more energised and be more productive at work, despite the many distractions, triggers and addictions of the modern workplace
- make fewer decisions from a place of fear and more from a place of confidence and heart
- become more self-aware, a better listener and more empathic, helping you connect with your team and internal and external customers in a more meaningful way
- increase the trust that those you serve (both internally and externally) have in you, and increase the value you bring
- reprogram your default behaviours to give you greater sustained results and create relationship-strengthening habits for life.

In this book, I ask you to soften, slow down and be gentler with people. I invite you to be less controlling and more convincing, less head and more heart, less outwardly focused and more inwardly focused. After all, service starts with you!

The practices I set out aren't theories or guesswork; they've improved thousands of people's relationships at work, with their customers and at home with their families and loved ones. This is a practical handbook on human relations in a world that demands service like never before.

HOW TO LEARN AND LEVERAGE NEW HABITS

There are differing views about how long it takes to embed a new habit. I like to follow Robin Sharma, one of the world's top leadership experts; when I visited Sharma at a leadership summit in Stockholm back in 2013, he told me that it takes 66 days to wire a new habit. The habit-installation process sees you go through three phases to reach what researchers call the 'automaticity point', where the habit feels easier and more automatic:

- *Phase one.* In the first 22 days, what Sharma calls 'destruction' occurs. You're destroying the old neural pathway in your mind, destroying an old habit, and it feels hard.

- *Phase two.* In the second period of 22 days, you experience confusion because the habit isn't yet automatic. You're growing, and you're disrupting your old habits, but you'll feel like giving up. It's important to stick with it in this messy middle phase.

- *Phase three.* In the final 22 days, the new habit is integrated and feels like a new way of being. It feels easy. You've wired new neural pathways in your mind and have reached automaticity with the new habit.

Sharma helped me to realise that installing habits takes time, and if you want to master something, you have to stick with it. I've kept this phased installation idea in mind for the past ten-plus years whenever I want to introduce a new habit, and have noticed that it happens every time.

A certain level of motivation is required to stick at something for 66 days – a commitment to making the change or improvement is paramount to you sticking with it. In addition, I do four things to make a new habit stick:

1. actively reflect
2. start somewhere
3. repeat, repeat, repeat
4. track progress.

I've created the following tools for these four things in the Service Habits offering – that is, this book and other associated resources – to help you establish new habits as easily as possible.

1. Reflection questions

To help you actively reflect, at the end of each chapter in the book is a series of questions under the heading 'Reflect now'. These are crafted to get you thinking about a habit more deeply and considering specifically what that habit means to you in your current work.

2. Embed the habit

Sometimes, not knowing where to start with a new habit is a barrier, so after the reflection questions I've included an 'Embed the habit' exercise to help you kick off.

3. The Service Habits program

You can't over-repeat the explanation and instructions for a new habit. So, to support you and your team further, we've created a premier training platform called the Service Habits program for individuals and organisations interested in embedding the service habits. The Service Habits program is an additional guide for those who want to reprogram their service habits and deepen the relationships with the people they serve immediately. With a variety of programs, online and face to face, the lessons are practical and the format is simple.

To learn more about the Service Habits program and various pathways, go to serviceq.co/programs.

4. The Service Habits Journal

The Service Habits Journal is a downloadable resource that makes it easy to track service habits in small chunks of time. It's a simple tool for recording whether you did a habit, and is designed for you to carry in your back pocket or bag or keep at your workstation, so it's never too far away.

The most common way to use a habit tracker like the journal is to focus on a few habits each month. The idea is to become aware of how well you're implementing these habits and stay consistent over time. You can choose which cluster of habits to focus on – or maybe your team or workplace is focusing on the same few habits each month to support each other?

To download the Service Habits Journal, go to bit.ly/TrackYour Habits.

• • •

Now, let's begin with Pillar 1: 'Know yourself'.

Pillar 1
KNOW YOURSELF

THE FIRST STEP to any transformation is awareness, and make no mistake: this book is a practical handbook for personal and professional transformation.

Service starts with you. Before you can even consider the customer, you need an awareness of how you show up and how present you are.

Self-awareness requires you to be present; the more present you are, the more chance you have of being self-aware. This is important in service because people experience you only in that moment. When you are present, and aware of how people experience you and react to your language, gestures and behaviours, you have a greater ability to develop skills that help you be your best professional self, moment to moment.

Working through these first seven habits is like sitting at the cinema and watching yourself in the movie of your life. They build on techniques of mindfulness and concentration awareness. By the time you get to the end of this first pillar, you will be:

· more conscious of the small choices you make at work and how they impact your mindset and behaviours

· more aware of the beliefs that support you

· more understanding of the implications of your thoughts and emotions

· more confident in managing your strong emotions and stress

· more aware of how people perceive you and open to feedback about your first impressions.

And hey, you might even have created a regular meditation practice!

Service Habit 1
CHOOSE TO SERVE

My favourite '90s movie is the Hollywood hit *Sliding Doors,* starring Gwyneth Paltrow as the lead character, Helen. The movie shows Helen living two parallel lives after a pivotal moment that changes everything.

One day, Helen gets sacked from her public relations job, leaves the office early and upset, and runs to catch the train. In this moment, she either makes the train or the door slides shut on her, leaving her standing on the empty platform. The two realities move forward: one sees Helen's life in a happy state and the other has her struggling through her days. (I won't tell you why; you'll have to watch the movie!) The movie is based on the idea that what seems like an insignificant moment on an ordinary day can set you on a different path.

Service is a lot like how this movie plays out. It all revolves around one pivotal moment: a person's initial interaction with you. The way you influence and interact with people every day – colleagues, customers, teammates, your boss – will set them on a path to either happiness or misery. No matter how small or insignificant human-to-human interactions may seem, how you treat people in each and every moment lingers for hours, days and weeks. It will be the reason why people come back, why people are happy to work with you or for you and, in some cases, why people leave you.

Relationships are formed through the many small interactions you have throughout a day. They craft a storyline that has a happy ending – or not. So, paying attention to the ordinary moments is critical to keeping the relationships that are dear to you on the path of happiness.

What may seem like an ordinary interaction to you may be a highlight for someone else. What felt like an insignificant moment for someone else may be a milestone moment for you. You never know what the person on the end of the phone, the other side of the counter or the other side of a meeting table may be going through. Your approach to serving people is a big deal.

> **When serving others, we must remember that ordinary days and insignificant moments matter most.**

In any moment, service is a choice: who you choose to be, how you choose to show up, what you choose to bring to that interaction. The first decision to make on the Service Habits journey is to **choose to serve**. So, what does choosing to serve look like?

99 PER CENT IS NOT 100 PER CENT

One of my meditation teachers says, '99 per cent committed is hard; 100 per cent committed is easy.'

What he means is that when you are 100 per cent committed to something, you are 'all in', unwavering – you aren't going to let anything come between you and your commitment. When you decide to be 100 per cent committed to the people you serve, you cut off any alternatives that may get in the way of that commitment. When you're only 99 per cent committed, by comparison, you're leaving 1 per cent to chance – a 1 per cent alternative – and this is why 100 per cent is easy: because there are no alternatives.

How would you feel if your partner or best friend came to you one day and said, 'I'm 99 per cent committed to you'? It would seem odd, wouldn't it; and you'd be left wondering, why only 99 per cent? You'd want more.

If you are giving anything less than full commitment in an interaction, it is obvious. I was once in a meeting with a new client – a meeting he had initiated – but his body language and behaviour told me he wasn't 100 per cent committed to the conversation. As soon as we sat down, I felt like he wanted to be someplace else. He was jittery, checking his watch; he didn't seem to be listening, and it felt like he was just going through the motions of the meeting to say that he'd done it. I left our interaction feeling unsure of whether I wanted to do business with him.

You can sense the vibe of someone only 99 per cent committed to you in a service environment. Like when you walk into a retail store or a restaurant just as they are about to close, and the employee greeting you seems almost disappointed you've arrived, because they were ready to go home. Someone who is 100 per cent committed would lean in, welcome you and show you in that moment that you are important to them.

When people give you, as a customer, less than 100 per cent of their commitment, they give you less than 100 per cent attention. You just know they're not fully present with you.

When you only give 99 per cent of your attention in service interactions, that missing 1 per cent can cost you:

- the trust of someone on your team
- a new client relationship
- a customer's sale.

People experience you moment by moment, and the mindset you choose to adopt in each and every moment is what determines your actions and behaviours. That 1 per cent requires you to pay attention to your small habits and behaviours. Service doesn't have to be big and grandiose to be meaningful, but you need to give 100 per cent of your attention – 99 per cent is not enough.

If someone or something is important enough to us, we'll always find a way to say yes and help them.

Michael Jordan has earnt the reputation of being one of the most incredible athletes on the planet. During his glory days, he was known for identifying the small moments and opportunities in a game. He would say, 'Once I made a decision, I never thought about it again.'

> **High performers of service are 100 per cent in – they don't leave the 1 per cent to chance.**

In the words of Derek Sivers, author of *Hell Yeah or No*, keep earning your title, or it will expire.

It requires daily practice to earn a title from your customers in business, such as 'they give great service', 'they are a good brand' or, 'they are my preferred choice'. Each day, when you open your doors, pick up the phone or pen an email, you must keep earning that title, just like Michael Jordan did with his approach to each game. In other words, you have to keep choosing to serve, each and every moment you are serving.

Check yourself now:

- What mindset do you choose in this moment?
- How committed are you to those you serve?
- Do you give people 100 per cent attention when you serve, eliminating any distractions that may get in the way of you listening?
- Do you take that extra phone call at 5 pm when you're due to finish, knowing it's a customer on the end of the line and hoping you can help them?

- Do you greet the last person who walks into your store at the end of the day with the same enthusiasm that you greeted the first person who walked into your store that day?

These are traits of someone who is choosing to serve – is this you?

A CONSCIOUS CHOICE

On any working day, you make conscious and unconscious choices about:

- what task to do next
- what to prioritise
- who to speak with about a problem
- when to speak with others and when to listen
- when to take a break.

When you make conscious choices, they get 100 per cent of your attention. This results in you having a certain aliveness about you – you're attentive, focused and committed to giving what it takes in that moment. As I mentioned earlier, if someone or something is important enough, you will always find a way to say yes or help them.

Unconscious choices, on the other hand, get less than 100 per cent of your attention. You can be easily charmed or distracted by something else, you're not fully present in that moment, and you may not be fully attentive to what you're experiencing. With unconscious choices, it's like you're on autopilot: mindless and certainly not present.

Customers or colleagues you serve, if asked, would probably say that they would appreciate your 100 per cent attention when you're with them. We all want to feel like we're important to others and that when someone is serving us, they are doing so fully and freely, not out of obligation. Fundamentally, we want to be served by people who consciously choose to do so.

You cannot serve and be self-absorbed at the same time.

Think of the moments in your life when someone has been there 100 per cent for you, in complete service to you. They may have helped you with a problem, given you a new perspective or allowed you to learn something new about yourself.

When you treat serving people as a chore, you can get lost and miss out the gifts and benefits that you, as the giver of service, can gain. Think about it:

- *Service not only raises questions, it gives you answers.* In a working environment in which circumstances and product demands are ever changing, information from your service interactions can be your secret weapon for staying innovative and relevant.

- *Service can help you drop your mask, connect with people and serve more from the heart.* When you serve from a place of authenticity, without a façade or mask, it is easier and takes less effort.

- *Service can help you understand people better.* The skills of service are skills for life. Understanding people strengthens leadership and good human-to-human behaviour, and every business that involves relationships needs people who can seek this understanding.

- *Service can still your restless mind.* Paying attention to others will turn down the volume on your self-dialogue. Many people seek, through daily mindfulness and meditation, to free their mind from thoughts of past or future events. When you're stressed and caught up in your thinking mind, one of the quickest ways to get out of your own head is to serve someone else and place your attention on them, in the now.

- *Service can fill you with joy and happiness – satisfaction that you've been useful to a fellow human being.* One of the basic needs of any human is self-esteem. There is a value exchange that comes from service besides products and money.

When you get out of your own way and truly step into a moment with someone, and you are there to listen, learn, help and serve, it's no longer about you. It's the ultimate gift to a fellow human being, to choose to serve them.

Lebanese poet Kahlil Gibran wrote in his poem 'On Work', 'Work is love made visible.' Our work in service can be part of our calling, part of our search for meaning and for why we exist. And I think in the heart of each of us, there's a desire to do good things in the world.

If you're in the service industry, then your mindset is what drives the quality of your performance as a service professional. It all starts with your level of commitment and what you choose to believe in each moment you are serving someone else.

So, do you choose to serve, or does your work feel like an obligation, a chore, or just a series of tasks?

This is the foundational habit for everything that follows. If you haven't chosen to be of service, it doesn't matter what other habits follow. Choose to serve, first.

Service Habit 1
CHOOSE TO SERVE

Reflect now

- Are you 100 per cent in for the people you say matter to you?
- How does that commitment transpire when you attend staff meetings, have corridor conversations with colleagues, serve customers and solve their problems?
- Who do you choose to be when you're at work?
    - Someone who leaves a positive impact every time they're with people?
    - Someone known for caring?
    - Someone known for giving people their time and attention?

Embed the habit

Choosing to serve is a daily choice. This is an invitation to bring some self-awareness and, for the next 24 hours, pay attention to what you are choosing in each moment of your day.

For the next 24 hours, choose to serve – wherever you are, whoever you are serving.

Notice what a conscious intention to choose to serve does to your mindset, your mood and the overall interaction between you and the person you are serving.

Service Habit 2
CREATE HELPFUL BELIEFS

Let's take a brief look at physics to see how beliefs can change significantly over time:

- In 1687, Sir Isaac Newton put forward the law of universal gravitation, which states that every particle attracts every other particle in the universe with a force that is directly proportional to the product of their masses.

- Then fast-forward to 1916, and Albert Einstein came up with the world's most famous equation, $E = mc^2$ (meaning, very roughly, that energy and mass are equivalent). Under this new theory, the 'belief' Newton had proposed about gravitation was kind of true, but kind of not true when you go fast.

- Then fast-forward again to Stephen Hawking in 1991, who said, 'Yeah, but what about the relativity of this? It's kind of not true at the beginning, and not true when things get really small.'

Physics tries to describe how the universe works (the 'ultimate truth', if you like) – and if that's constantly being revised and updated with new ideas, then it's kind of crazy to believe our own smaller beliefs are true and final. So, rather than viewing beliefs as either true or untrue, choose to see them as helpful or unhelpful.

This habit is about self-awareness – seeing whether a certain belief is good for you and supports you to be your best professional self, or not – and doing something about it. The story you tell yourself is everything.

Beliefs are like coloured-lens glasses: they are subtle, but they influence how you see the world. And you don't realise it until you take off the glasses and see their colours!

Your beliefs can either stand in the way of your success or become the foundation for it.

Let's examine how helpful beliefs about service can best support you.

BELIEFS TURN INTO ACTIONS

In his book *Useful Belief: Because it's better than positive thinking*, author Chris Helder explains the power of beliefs and how they impact your actions. There is an important part of your brain called the reticular activating system that works as a type of filter – it shows you what you want to see. For example, if you decide to look for red cars tonight on your way home, you will notice more red cars, because you have told your brain to look for them. Likewise, if you tell yourself that today is going to be a terrible day, your brain goes looking for facts to support this idea. It's like you send your brain on a fact-finding mission.

Think about something you once believed to be true but which you don't believe anymore. How helpful would it be to hold onto that belief? How would that impact you at work, and people you interact with?

UNHELPFUL VERSUS HELPFUL BELIEFS

A question you can ask yourself about your beliefs that might help create the change or growth you seek is: 'Is it helpful?'

To test your level of commitment to the relationships in your workplace, it's useful to test your beliefs. What you choose to believe – your mindset, your judgements, your set of assumptions and your relationship to service – is the most powerful influence on how others experience you when you serve them.

The following table lists the most common beliefs about service. Which do you identify with?

Table 1: Common beliefs about service

Unhelpful service beliefs	Helpful service beliefs
Serving people is a chore.	Serving people is an honour.
I'm right and you're wrong.	I'm here to solve problems and find solutions.
I'm here to make money.	I'm here to make meaning.
I'm not good with people.	I'm learning to understand people.
I know what you want.	I seek to understand what you want.
I don't serve customers.	I know I have an impact on customers.
Service is not my job.	Service is everybody's responsibility.
It's my job to serve customers.	It's a joy to serve people.

Look at the unhelpful beliefs first. They're called 'unhelpful' because, while they're not wrong or evil, they will get in the way of being 100 per cent committed to serving someone. If you identify with any of these unhelpful beliefs, or you know someone in your team who does, then consider that those beliefs will:

· limit your potential to impact other humans positively

· create unnecessary friction and barriers in interaction with others

· make it feel like you're making unnecessary effort

· make it harder, because you have chosen not to care enough in the first place to do what it takes in the face of setbacks.

How would someone who had one or many of the unhelpful service beliefs behave and serve? What would the quality of their actions and service habits be like, and how would it feel to be on the receiving end of it?

On the other hand, helpful beliefs are not necessarily perfect or right, but they will support your commitment and mindset to giving people 100 per cent of your attention. If you choose to be in the service industry, it will be more helpful if you conduct yourself from a place of helpful beliefs. They will:

· impact other humans in a way that is expansive and positive

· allow you to connect more easily with people and have seamless interactions

· make work feel effortless

· minimise conflict and friction when serving people.

The best part about beliefs is that a belief need not be true. You choose to believe, and you can change what you believe at any time. Typically, your beliefs have been influenced by factors such as your environment, the workplace culture you're in, role models in your life, your leaders, past experiences, where you were raised and where you have worked before. If you want to reframe some of the unhelpful beliefs to be more helpful, you have that choice – you can choose whether you keep a belief or not.

Evaluate whether a belief is helpful or not, rather than whether it's true.

MAKE BELIEVE

Sometimes we need to 'act as if' we are already being something, doing something or have obtained a goal we desire in order to make it a reality. The principle of 'acting as if' was first written about a century ago by William James, a philosopher and trained physician. He coined the phrase and outlined how to create motivation to do things that you're reluctant to do.

I remember adopting this principle as a young crew member at McDonald's. I aspired to be a manager, so I watched the way the managers dressed, walked, spoke to staff and conducted themselves in the dining room; what they paid attention to when they walked through the kitchen; how they spoke to customers; even what they chose to eat on their lunchbreaks. I watched very closely their manner, facial expressions, tone, pace and posture. I knew that they were successful, so I acted like them – until one day, I was just like them.

If you want to be successful at service, you must act, talk and think like a successful service person.

So, who do you know who is always behaving with a service mindset? What is it that they say and do? How do they go about their day, their tasks? This is a helpful way of seeing clearly what 'good' looks like, and imitating it – being inspired by it – to the point where you feel you can do it in your own authentic way. This is the first step towards adopting a service mindset.

CREATE HELPFUL BELIEFS

Reflect now

- What do you choose to believe?
- How helpful are your beliefs about service, and do they support you to be your best professional self?
- Where have you been most influenced by your beliefs of service?
- What service beliefs are you changing?

Embed the habit

1. Get clear about the unhelpful and helpful beliefs that are feeding your service mindset. Refer to table 1 on page 23 for prompts, and check in with any beliefs you have about service that aren't listed in the table.

2. Once you've decided what you believe to be true about service, start to write on sticky notes the new beliefs that you think will be helpful for stepping into a service mindset. For example, 'I believe that I'm here to make a difference to people each day.'

3. Place the sticky notes somewhere you'll see them often.

4. Read them every day for 21 days.

5. After the 21 days, reflect on how you feel about that belief. Notice the change in yourself.

Service Habit 3
TAKE FOUR SECONDS

In 2005, I was working in London when my career took an exciting turn: I joined the leadership team in charge of mobilising the rebuild of Wembley National Stadium. It was going to be the biggest stadium in the world at the time, with 100,000 seats in the stadium and corporate dining that could accommodate up to 10,000 people at one time in the restaurants and suites (hard to imagine now in a post-pandemic world). I was responsible for the corporate dining areas, which boasted the latest technology and promised high-end restaurant food uncharacteristic of a stadium environment. My customer group was made up of celebrities, high-flying millionaires, reputable business leaders and global sports personalities.

As we geared up to open the stadium, I was really starting to feel the pressure – in fact, I've never felt pressure in my career like I did during that time. The opening was delayed by two years, so the expectations of performance were amplified and customer expectations inflated. People were dying to get in to see the finished stadium and entertain their guests in one of the new dining areas.

I was aware that:

- my performance was under scrutiny, as I had never managed this size team before

- the pressure of delivering world-class hospitality to millionaires and global celebrities was immense – customers had expectations that I had never encountered before
- everything was new – the stadium, the equipment, the menu, the team. There were so many 'what ifs' and 'maybes' that it really was a highly intense operational environment.

On the outside, I was performing at an optimum level, hitting all the goals I was set; but on the inside, I was suffering from anxiety, struggling to adjust to a new international home life and juggling the challenges of a highly intense workplace.

I became very reactive with my team. I found myself continually buried in my to-do list, focused purely on what needed doing. I would bark out orders, direct and instruct, allowing very little space or time for others' input. I rushed from meeting to meeting, very organised on paper and ticking things off the to-do list, but unaware of how I was treating people who were also feeling the pressure.

I was incredibly invested in the success of my team and the opening of the stadium. This was what I had lived and breathed for three years: I'd uprooted my life for the stadium, and I couldn't see how much meaning I was giving to the small, insignificant things in a day. I'd lost perspective.

I found out that people were describing me as 'stressed out' and 'too emotional'. I was having a negative impact on those around me, and my kneejerk reactions were damaging my relationships and reputation with the team. I felt like a jack-in-the-box that had been wound up so tightly it might burst out at any moment, and I was addicted to getting stuff done quickly. I needed everything to be quicker – staff to work faster and problems to be resolved faster. I didn't yet have great tools like the ones I'm sharing with you in this book.

This service habit (like all of the service habits) has no expiration date. In 2005 and today, we are all at risk of matching our service style to the erratic, fast-paced modern-day environment, so that the last thing we think to do is slow down... yet that's exactly what is needed.

THE NEED FOR SPEED

The need for speed in a service environment is obvious. Nowadays, customers drive this agenda and expect companies to create systems, processes and technology that provide them with solutions as quickly as possible. This need for speed has perpetuated since 2019 with the global pandemic. The expectation to pivot, innovate and be agile and flexible in the face of uncertainty and an ongoing crisis leaves people in service roles feeling more out of control than in control. As a result, if you serve customers directly or lead a team that serves customers, you will more than likely have formed the habit of moving from one customer to the next very quickly and, in some cases, mindlessly.

The need for speed, although it addresses productivity, puts the quality of service interactions at risk. You can be thrown off-centre in a matter of moments. All it takes is:

- an error by a colleague that just cost you more time and money
- an influx of customers who all want something now
- an overwhelming to-do list and not enough people to get the work done.

When any or all of these stressful, intense and urgent situations occur, the sympathetic nervous system is activated and prepares the body for a fight. In other words, your survival mechanism kicks in and increases your heart rate, blood pressure and blood sugar. It's termed a 'fight-or-flight response': an evolutionary reaction to immediate danger.

Stadium environments, just like many other workplace environments, have a certain intensity about them. Safety, risk, people movement and people management are all under scrutiny. Often, I say to my stadium clients that they are continually living in a state of fight or flight when they come to work. They are on high alert and their nervous system is wired, and they are expected to perform at their peak under these conditions.

We are not meant to operate in a constant state of fight or flight, though: we are not wired for this. Just like birds are not wired to see glass windows and kangaroos are not wired to stop at freeways where cars are zooming past. When our nervous system is under pressure, we have less control of our own reactivity in moments that matter.

The issue is that if we serve from a place of fight or flight, we may:

· say things without thinking them through

· make decisions that are emotionally charged and not objective enough for what or who is most important

· deliver words and actions in a manner tinged with resentment or obligation

· come across as someone who panics or is a 'stress head', creating doubt in the people we work with and the people we work for (our customers).

Our desire to speed through a day feeds our distractions and triggers exhaustion. It affects our state of awareness in the moment and clouds our thoughts, judgements and perspectives. It makes it hard to give considered responses when serving others.

When you are distracted, exhausted, triggered and addicted to work, your service to others can feel harder than it needs to be.

STOP REACTING

Sometimes you might not like how you come across or how you've behaved when interacting with someone, but you feel that you weren't able to catch that thought or emotion in time. If you lead a team, you may notice that, when you're under pressure, it's easier to give orders and tell people what to do instead of asking questions and encouraging input. You may even be short with people when you're frustrated or disappointed (how human of you) and allow those emotions to be seen by your team, which creates more angst and is not helpful for moving through the situation.

If you're a member of a team that serves customers all day, it's easy to become complacent and short-sighted about the way you're treating customers. You may notice you only say the bare minimum when interacting, or perhaps you adopt a tone or have a look on your face that tells the customer you're not that interested in them and their problem or needs. Regardless of whether you're a leader or frontline employee, it's easy to slip into an unconscious state throughout the day and become unaware of how you're behaving.

Are you reacting or responding? Reacting is acting without conscious thought. Responding is acting consciously and intentionally.

When you notice you're speeding up, rushing tasks and moving through interactions unconsciously, it's time to do what feels counterproductive: slow down. When you rush, you miss indicators from colleagues and customers – indicators that are critical for providing them with the service response that they need in that moment. When you slow down, you allow yourself time to observe and see a situation for what it is.

This service habit, 'Take four seconds', empowers you to make a choice: will you meet challenges with reactivity or with equanimity? If you choose equanimity, the fastest way to gain that is to breathe.

LEARNING TO BREATHE

To cope with the pressure I was feeling in the build-up to Wembley National Stadium opening, I started going to yoga. This is where I learned something that's now one of my most valuable tools in coping with situations like this: how to breathe consciously.

When we're born into this world, we naturally start breathing. We're not taught to breathe consciously or shown how to breathe to benefit ourselves – we do it naturally, effortlessly, without giving it another thought. However, I couldn't get over how quickly and deeply the practice of yoga breathing changed the way I was thinking or feeling. I began to intentionally practise breathing outside of the yoga studio, at work and in meetings. My breath helped melt away any angst or stress, like fire melts ice.

Let me give you an example. I remember a day when I was conducting a briefing with my team of managers. We had a huge task ahead of us on this day, and the team arrived anticipating my usual bossy approach. Before I opened the briefing, though, I did some slow awareness breathing to bring my attention to my breath and take me away from my racing mind. I recall feeling super calm, and the way my team responded was incredibly positive. People felt comfortable to ask questions and provide input – input and questions that proved extremely beneficial to how we approached the day.

When I began to understand how to consciously control my breath to calm my nervous system down, the effects were transformational.

Breathing consciously is like a drug. As Max Strom, author of *A Life Worth Breathing*, says, 'We know alcohol and drugs can calm us down, but what most people don't realise is that the nervous system can be brought into harmony through breathing techniques, and with zero side effects.'

The goal of breathing consciously is to wake us up in that moment, to become self-aware, so that we can act more consciously.

Breathing helps you see things differently and make new choices based on this new vision.

Four seconds is all it takes

The breath is the bridge between the body and the mind, which enables you to get self-aware and act consciously. It's a skill to develop awareness of when you are stressed at work and notice how it affects those around you. Once you notice what you don't like, the breath is the very first tool you can reach for to adjust your next move. When you intentionally start to breathe, this supports the parasympathetic nervous system (PSNS), quiets the mind and helps to bring about a state of more focused attention.

Let's face it – we're much more relaxed and at ease when the people around us are relaxed and at ease. Ask yourself these questions:

· Would you rather talk to someone who panics and gets reactive when things go wrong, or to someone who knows how to stay calm and positive even amid difficulty?

· Would you rather work with someone who's hot and cold, and erratic, or someone who's fairly consistent and considered with their responses, each and every time?

If the latter person in each instance is the kind you'd rather be with, chances are your colleagues and customers feel the same way. The good news is that, as quickly as you can be thrown off-centre into a state of chaos or panic, you can come back to a place that is calmer and more considered.

In his book *Four Seconds*, Peter Bregman writes, '[A] short pause is all you need to see where you're going wrong and to make a little shift.' Realistically, we often don't have time to do long breathing exercises at work (and it would probably look a little funny!), but it only takes four seconds to take a breath. Inhaling for two seconds and exhaling for two seconds decreases activity in your nervous system and triggers a relaxation response within you. It sends a signal to the PSNS that lowers heart rate and blood pressure and brings you more into a 'rest and digest' mode. (It's primarily during rest, eating and sleeping that the PSNS dominates, to coordinate the body's repose and regeneration.)

You can manage and control your reactions in four seconds, in four steps:

1. First, notice when you're thinking or feeling in a way that may not be helpful when interacting with those around you.

2. Once you've noticed this, you can take a pause – a short pause, just long enough to take one deep breath in from your belly. This helps activate the PSNS.

3. The third step is critical: to slow your reactions down, after you've invited a breath in, then you need to slowly and consciously breathe out.

4. This provides just enough time to catch your thought and, with a quieter, more relaxed mind, to make a better decision when responding to the person or people in front of you.

One of the mistakes that people make with this exercise is that they think it's about counting to four – like when you were naughty as a kid, and you were asked to sit in the corner and count to ten. As effective as counting might be to create some space, what you're really practising is the breathing, not the counting. Try it now: all it takes is four seconds to pause, breathe and course-correct!

TAKE FOUR SECONDS

Reflect now

- How conscious are you of your breathing? Have you noticed how it impacts your thinking, decision-making and judgements?
- What would the consequence of slowing down your response by four seconds be? Would people notice?
- Where and when do you think this service habit will be most useful for you?

Embed the habit

The goal of the four-second breath is to slow things down slightly and give you an opportunity to make a course-correction in the conversation or task you're engaged in. I've worked with thousands of professionals in the service industry, and some of the most popular times people choose to use this service habit are:

- during meetings
- in between serving customers
- when dealing with a complaint or difficult conversation
- before presenting to a group
- any time they feel nervous or off-centre, or when strong emotions and thoughts are taking over.

Choose a situation that you feel you'd benefit from approaching with a clearer head, and start practising four-second breaths.

Service Habit 4
WATCH YOUR THOUGHTS

The train drivers on the Beijing–Shanghai high-speed railway, one of the world's busiest railways, are required to wear electro-encephalography (EEG) devices in their helmets to monitor their brain activity while driving.

The drivers are carrying thousands of passengers every day on their trains, and for safety reasons, the data captured is being used to reassign workers who zone out, or show emotional agitation or less-than-stellar concentration on the job.

We don't have the benefit of an EEG device monitoring our thoughts, so it is up to us to watch them and notice when we zone out and lose concentration.

The reality is that we do often see people lose concentration at work, and when it involves another person, it can send a message that can damage the relationship, such as:

· 'I'm not interested in you.'
· 'I'm bored with serving you.'
· 'I have other things to do.'
· 'I'm not really focused; there are more important things on my mind.'

When we're on the receiving end of service from someone lacking in concentration, we often don't call it out because we're only going on a hunch, a sense, a feeling. What if we could read people's minds, though, and see exactly what they're thinking? Would we have better conversations? Would we be more disciplined with our thoughts and find ways to keep our minds on the job so as not to offend or upset anyone?

As scary as it may be in terms of privacy, I think it's an interesting concept to consider when interacting with customers and colleagues. It's estimated that a human mind thinks at least 2000 thoughts an hour. So, unless you are in a coma or deep sleep, your mind is on and you're always thinking. However, is your mind always on the job? If not, what impact does this have on the people you serve?

HELP VERSUS HINDER

Great service happens when we are in the present moment. What typically takes us away from the 'now' are thoughts about the past or future.

This can be unhelpful and divert our attention from the person in front of us. Unhelpful thoughts:

- are irrelevant at that moment
- direct our energy and concern to something that just happened or is about to happen
- may be judgemental or critical about someone or something.

When you think these sorts of thoughts, you find that while you're present in body, you're not present in mind. You often see this kind of absentminded service in business. It's transactional and shallow, and it feels like the person being served isn't the primary object of the server's attention.

Helpful thoughts, on the other hand:

· are relevant to the moment
· are non-judgemental and open-minded
· give greater energy to what's happening now.

While thoughts are inevitable and we can't predict them, we can become aware of them and practise keeping our minds on the job.

WHAT DO YOU THINK?

The mind loves to swim in thoughts of the past or future. It is addicted to thinking, and its primary purpose is to get your attention and make sure you are listening. You may notice that you often focus your energy and attention on a past experience or past thought. For example, you might say to a returning customer, 'Hi there! Welcome back, and great to see you again,' but be thinking, 'Oh, you're that lady who gave me grief last time you were here... to be honest, I'm not really happy to see you.'

You may also notice that you direct your energy and attention to future thoughts – anticipating something that hasn't happened yet. For example, you might say to a customer, 'I hope you have a great day,' but be thinking, 'I'm so hungry; I can't wait for my lunch break.'

The problem with past and future thoughts is that they take you away from the now: they drag your attention away from who and what is in front of you. The colleague or customer you're interacting with may well sense you're not really present – if they could read your mind, it would no doubt cost you money and a returning customer, not to mention make you feel ashamed and humiliated! You'll have heard the expression 'I can hear what you're thinking'; while people can't read your thoughts, you will give off a vibe or energy that isn't fully in sync with your words.

When our words aren't congruent with our thoughts, people sense it.

So, how do we catch these thoughts when they appear, and what's a useful way of dealing with them so we don't damage our relationships?

BECOMING TRANSPARENT

The best service is delivered by someone who really means what they say – there's a genuineness about their care and one-on-one attention. Their words are congruent with their thoughts, behaviours and actions.

People who deliver transparent service gain the trust of others very quickly.

If others could read our thoughts, then maybe we would:

· be more determined to manage our thoughts

· have healthier minds

· have braver and more honest conversations

· understand more and guess less

· think about and judge others less.

Ask yourself two questions:

1. How helpful is this thought for this moment right now?
2. If this person could read my mind, would I continue this train of thought?

The good news is that you can control the quality of your thoughts, the thinking patterns you have on repeat, the beliefs you choose to hold and the volume of thoughts you allow. Just like Service Habit #2, 'Create helpful beliefs', your thoughts can support you or get in the way of you being your best professional self.

Consider the example we ran through before, where you say to a customer, 'I hope you have a great day,' but your thought is, 'I'm so hungry and can't wait to have a break.' You can choose to *ask that thought to leave* by simply saying in your mind, 'That's not a helpful thought for me to be having right now: please go.'

With the returning customer who you're not really happy to see you can choose to *reframe this thought* by simply saying to yourself, 'Oh, you're the lady who left upset last time; let me see if we can get onto common ground today.'

You can choose to be in the driver's seat of your mind: it's simply a commitment and a practice of building strength in the mind, just like going to the gym to train and build muscle.

Let's look at an easy and memorable process for building greater strength around watching your thoughts and seeing how helpful they are for you and those around you.

THE THREE CS: CATCH IT, CHECK IT, CORRECT IT

Catch it

Awareness is the first step in any transformation. You have to be aware of your thoughts to be able to make them support you. So, this first step is to catch the thoughts in the moment – like you are catching a thought bubble hovering over your head.

I call this the 'catch it' step. Recognising an unhelpful thought is the hardest part. The next two steps are easy.

Check it

Once you have caught the thought, you are able to see how helpful it is or is not. Ask yourself, 'Is this a helpful thought in this situation, or not?'

The aim here is to look for the good in the situation that you've chosen to ignore or that you haven't yet seen, to widen your perspective.

Be very objective and ask yourself questions such as:

- What if this wasn't bad news?
- What good could come from this?
- How else might people choose to see this?

The 'check it' step may take some time, or you may get answers immediately.

Correct it

The final step is to 'correct it'. The word 'correct' can imply that something is broken and needs fixing, but I'd rather think of it in the sense of correcting course, which is more positive. You adjust your thoughts to be more in line with the truth of the whole situation: the light sides as well as the negative parts. Ask yourself:

- Can I allow space for what's happening right now, without trying to control the situation?
- Can I be okay with the hard and messy aspects of this situation?
- Is there another way to approach this?

• • •

The three Cs process helps you be uber-aware of your thoughts. This can be enough! It will mean you are well and truly on the path to being present and in the moment with people you serve.

Additionally, if you're paying attention to your thoughts when a difficult situation presents itself, you can avoid forming bad thinking habits that will have a negative impact on both your ability to cope and most certainly on the way you treat people. Three of the most common unhelpful thinking styles are:

1. *overgeneralising* – seeing a pattern based upon a single event, or drawing overly broad conclusions

2. *mental filtering* – only paying attention to certain types of evidence; for example, noticing failures but not seeing successes

3. *disqualifying the positive* – dismissing the good things that have happened as if they simply don't count.

When used regularly, the three Cs will help you build more muscle around managing unhelpful thinking habits and, ultimately, helping your thoughts help you during all the moments in service.

Service Habit 4
WATCH YOUR THOUGHTS

Reflect now

- What do you do when your mind drifts? How do you come back?

- What do you think is felt or experienced by another person when you are with them in body but your thoughts are somewhere else?

- How do you stay focused on, and aware of, the people you're interacting with, as opposed to your unspoken thoughts?

Embed the habit

Imagine you're wearing a hat or helmet fitted with an EEG device that monitors your thoughts and emotions. Just like in the movie *Sliding Doors* (mentioned in chapter 1), small changes such as your attention waning and your thoughts drifting can have big results. However, you're the director of your mind – you just need to pay attention and catch your thoughts to be able to direct them.

So, play, get curious and notice your thoughts:

- *Check in with yourself often.* When you get distracted by your own inner dialogue and the thinking mind becomes louder than any other noise around you, notice the internal chatter and acknowledge it.

- *Turn the volume down.* Without judgement, ask an unhelpful thought to leave, or reframe it. If it chooses not to leave your mind, however, then allow it to hover and perhaps find a way to turn the volume down on it a little.

Service Habit 5
MEDITATE DAILY

Do you ever experience overwhelm? Of course you do; you're human! At work, overwhelm usually occurs because we feel like we don't have enough hours in the day to do what we want or need to do. It's a result of ever-increasing expectations to get more done more quickly, especially of leaders. It seems like there's always something more to do. Weekdays are full of reports, after-work activities, social events or sport. Weekends are full of family time, more sport, more social events and getting on top of chores and domestic duties.

Can you relate to this? I certainly can. If you're working in a fast-paced environment where you are serving people all day (whether internal or external customers), chances are you get very little 'non-doing' time. Because you're running so fast to keep up with your schedule and to get things done, sometimes you feel like you're running on empty, with no time to catch your breath and no space for being still with no agenda. By 'no agenda', I don't mean distracting yourself with your phone, snacking, conversing with others or daydreaming. I'm talking about resting aware-ness – spending deep time resting in alertness, with the mind spacious and open.

As the philosopher Lao Tzu said, 'By non-doing, all doing becomes possible'.

BUSY AND EXHAUSTED

When you have a busy mind, particularly when you serve people, your mind is scattered and unfocused, paying attention to many things other than what you're doing. A busy mind is often termed the 'monkey mind' – the wandering mind that jumps from one thought to the next. It's addicted to doing and thinking; it wanders off and is easily distracted by irrelevant pieces of information.

You know you have a monkey mind when you:

· get agitated easily

· find your thinking isn't clear or you can't pay attention for long periods of time

· feel that your mind is overcrowded and you need some mind space

· feel overwhelmed by your work to-do list and your life to-do list, and don't know where to start some days

· receive feedback that you need to listen more or be more empathic.

A busy mind combined with a busy work life is a recipe for greater distractions, stress and anxiety.

Regardless of the service environment you work in, the pace of life and the demands of the modern-day world act as barriers for us humans to being mindful and thinking clearly when dealing with other humans.

Take a straightforward work environment like a call centre as an example. The staff have to sit at a desk with a headset on and talk to hundreds of customers per day! Now add to that the number of customer complaints they're taking on those calls, and sheer exhaustion makes it a tough gig.

How likely is it that, if you were a call centre worker, you would be able to serve everyone with the same fresh mind and enthusiasm you had with your first customer or colleague of the day? How do you stay mindful when the monkey mind is active and there are many people to serve?

MINDFUL SERVICE

Good service is about maintaining your energy and your state of mind over a long period of time. The art is in allowing situations (which are often out of your control) to reveal themselves, and when they do, maintaining presence while serving customer after customer and colleague after colleague in the best, clearest state of mind possible.

You're human after all, not a robot, and your advantage over robots – having emotions and thoughts – is also your biggest threat if you're unable to manage those thoughts and emotions when serving many people. You have to manage the ebb and flow of energy and motivation in between each customer interaction or internal meeting, over the day and for the long term. When you manage these cycles rather than ignore them, you're far more productive, happier and less drained.

Regardless of whether you're having a good day or a bad day, whether you're at the beginning of your shift or the end, whether it's a Monday or a Friday, the human being you're serving wants to feel like they're the first person you've served that day. Your job is to make them believe this, whether they're an internal customer, a colleague or a paying customer – you have the greatest impact on those you serve when you're fully present in every moment of a workday.

Think about those busy call centres. When we're talking to a script-reader, we feel like they're going through the motions, mindlessly performing a routine task. The ability to stay in the present and deal with challenges in service interactions is an asset. This very simple idea of giving moment-to-moment attention to others with a non-judgemental mind is not so easy to implement, though, when you serve many people throughout a day. Being mindful is the key to high performance in a service role.

Being mindful means that you:

- actively notice new things – this is critical in a service role when you're trying to read people and meet their needs

- stay present and keep things in perspective – crucial when you're dealing with grumpy customers and complaints

- turn the volume down on the mindless, negative chit-chat that makes you worry and stress unnecessarily, helping you to conserve mental energy throughout a day

- are emotionally agile – that is, you have self-control and empathy, so you can read people's needs and try to understand them

- judge others less, so that you appreciate people for who they are and make everyone feel special.

Mindfulness is essential for navigating the chaos – but the chaos makes it a lot harder to be mindful. According to a 2016 *Harvard Business Review* article called 'How to practice mindfulness throughout your work day', research showed that people spend nearly 47 per cent of their waking hours thinking about something other than what they're doing – operating on autopilot.

Mindfulness, by contrast, is defined by expert Jon Kabat-Zinn as 'paying attention in a particular way: on purpose, in the present moment, and nonjudgmentally'. It's the work that you do to retrain concentration so you're present with what is, and untrain distractions that aren't helpful or relevant to that present situation.

The most extraordinary service comes from people who are extraordinarily present.

TRAIN THE BRAIN

So, how do we retrain the brain? Meditation is my preferred method. Meditation leads to mindfulness.

When the mind is concentrated on the present moment in meditation, habitual thought patterns lose their power, and judging, projections, being lost in thought and making assumptions are all suspended. It's like going to the gym; just as workouts are the training needed to achieve a fit body, meditation is the training needed to achieve mindfulness.

Regular running will mean you're able to run further. Regular weight training will mean that eventually you'll be stronger. In the same way, committing to mental training will help you gain greater mental abilities, such as reprogramming the brain to be more rational and less emotional. Mental training enables you to stay relaxed and alert at the same time.

Meditation is one form of mental training. I personally approach it as I would a morning cup of coffee – the difference being that a morning meditation (my mental training) keeps me energised for the full day without caffeine. Starting the day with a 20-minute meditation practice activates my PSNS and releases energy, boosting endorphins that wake me up and making me more enthusiastic and fresh all day long. Meditation promotes mental balance by controlling the monkey mind, and makes for an incredibly productive day.

An analogy that has been used for 2700 years in Buddhist teachings is that the mind is like a container of water full of sediment.

Imagine that you're constantly shaking this container so that the water appears cloudy – this symbolises the monkey mind in full flight. Then, imagine you stop shaking the container and put it down. The silt settles to the bottom, and after a while the water becomes calm and clear. This illustrates what happens during meditation.

Three qualities emerge when the mind is in a meditative state: calmness, clarity and happiness. When you're calm, clear and happy, you can fight momentary urges that are not conducive to remaining alert and mindful. How many times in a day do you get an urge to do something that isn't helpful when you're in a service role?

- To daydream while you're waiting for a customer to walk into a store?
- To scroll through social media in the middle of your day?
- To take six tea breaks in one day to avoid a difficult conversation you need to have?

You can make intentional choices about which urges to follow and which to let pass. Mental training gives you power to control this.

Mental training naturally makes you more productive by increasing your capacity to resist distracting urges.

There's a reason that Google offers its employees a free meditation course: 'Search Inside Yourself'! A 2015 *Harvard Business Review* article called 'Mindfulness can literally change your brain' detailed a study that the *Review* conducted on meditation, and explained that meditation trains a part of your brain called the anterior cingulate cortex (ACC). The ACC is located deep inside the forehead behind the brain's frontal lobe and is 'associated with self-regulation, meaning the ability to purposefully direct attention and behavior, suppress knee-jerk responses, and switch strategies flexibly'. The study found that meditators demonstrated superior performance on self-regulation tests, resisting distractions and providing correct answers more often than non-meditators.

You can have all the best service training and all the tools and resources you need, but the truth is, none of that is going to help you if you're stuck in your head. The ability to maintain attention and focus is just as important as technical or management skills. The customer doesn't care how many other people you've served that day, so you need to learn how to stay present and find ways to reset before serving them.

Also, customers enjoy being served by employees who appear to be well – well physically, mentally and emotionally.

MEDITATION LEADS TO WELLBEING

Never before has there been such a focus on mental health and emotional wellbeing in the workplace. Meditation is becoming more mainstream – it's taught in universities and workplaces, and practised by high-level managers, politicians and sports stars. It's not really surprising, given the many health and wellbeing benefits of a regular meditation practice – including, for example:

- *better control of your emotions* – a study published in *Frontiers in Human Neuroscience* found that meditation might have a lasting effect on the amygdala, the part of the brain that processes emotion

- *potent anti-ageing effects* – studies from the *International Journal of Neuroscience* found that short-term meditators had a biological age five years younger than similarly aged non-meditators. Long-term meditators had an average biological age reduction of 12 years compared to non-meditators.

And here are a bunch of other reasons why meditation leads to wellbeing that you may want to look into yourself:

- It increases positive emotion.
- It decreases anxiety.
- It increases social connection.
- It increases brain power.
- It improves memory.
- It increases the ability to sleep more deeply and for longer.
- It decreases the incidence of heart disease via stress reduction.
- It helps to maintain healthy blood pressure.
- It helps reduce addictions.

To provide stand-out service, you and your teammates must have a positive mindset, feel engaged, be attentive and, ultimately, be happy to give the best possible service you can. When you're met with challenges and problems, you can cope and maintain this mental clarity and positivity with the help of meditation.

MENTAL FITNESS

There are four reasons that those who meditate or do some form of mental training are often stand-out service leaders and team members:

1. *Better self-control.* Sometimes people may say or do things you don't agree with, but when you practise meditation, it gives you a peacefulness that you can return to when things feel out of control. If you lead a team, this will give your employees confidence in your decision-making and a sense that you're approachable. In the same way, team members who display good self-control give customers a sense of confidence.

2. *Improved concentration.* From my own experience of spending time with those who meditate and those who do not, meditators focus better on their work and are more productive, with heightened attention and concentration spans. Both customers and teammates benefit from the clarity and promptness of their service, and their lower error rate and greater efficiency.

3. *Mental clarity.* Meditators are more able to make good decisions. Studies have revealed that mindful meditation practices improve the brain's problem-solving and decision-making abilities, and customers and colleagues will benefit from feeling that they're in the hands of a smart, knowledgeable employee.

4. *Enhanced emotional intelligence and empathy.* Meditation fires neural connections that regulate positive traits like empathy and kindness. Meditators can put themselves in someone else's shoes and assess situations with compassion for others, which makes them more amicable. Customers and colleagues will feel a better connection with the employee as a result.

TOO BUSY TO MEDITATE?

We are all busy, and many people I speak with in our meditation workshops believe that they don't have time to meditate. It almost feels counterintuitive to sit still for a period of time and do nothing when there is so much to do! I get it. Let's be clear: meditating is not going to make your schedule any less hectic; but, as mentioned earlier, it will allow you to move through the day and respond to your busy life in a far more grounded way.

There's an old Zen adage: 'You should sit in meditation for 20 minutes every day. Unless you're too busy – then you should sit for an hour.' At first, that doesn't make a whole lot of sense; but anybody who's had a meditation practice will say, 'I totally get it!' Meditation is anything but a waste of time: in fact, it buys you time. It's the best tool for building the muscle you need for mindfulness and bringing attention to the present moment.

Before we move on from this point, take a moment to consider this: there are 1440 minutes in the day. How many of these minutes do you spend watching TV, scrolling through social media or getting lost in online entertainment? Devoting a few minutes a day to yourself for meditation, by comparison, is a worthwhile investment in your wellbeing.

MEDITATE YOUR WAY

So, how do you meditate? If you're just starting, keep it very simple. Here are three different styles to experiment with: walking meditation, micro-meditation and 'bum-on-cushion' meditation.

1. Walking meditation

Before you start walking, stand still. Notice your breath and pay attention to the soles of your feet evenly weighted on the ground. Then, take a step forward and lift one foot mindfully, shifting your weight as you plant the foot down and then step with the other foot.

I like to follow my breath when I walk, saying silently to myself 'inhale' and 'exhale'. You could, instead, silently say 'lifting' when you lift a foot and 'moving' when you move forward. Doing this will help inject alertness and calmness into the experience.

2. Micro-meditation

I am a firm believer that the length of time you spend in meditation is less important than the habit of doing it daily. Five minutes a day is better than nothing: the key is to meditate daily. Some days, micro-meditation is all I have time for.

I like to do micro-meditations when I'm:

- shifting from one phone call to another
- having back-to-back client meetings
- walking from one meeting room into the next
- walking outside to get some lunch.

I do this sometimes when I'm sitting in the car before an appointment, when I'm in my office in between busy periods and when I'm travelling in planes and on trams. Some of my clients have shared with me that they do micro-meditations most:

- in the car between sales calls or visits
- at the airport terminal visiting different retail shop managers
- before a site visit.

For a micro-meditation, follow these steps:

1. Notice how your body feels.
2. How are you breathing? Notice how deep or shallow your breathing is.
3. Then, take a deep breath from the belly and let it go. Keep following your breath, the inhale and exhale, and pay attention to the rhythm. If you need to, it sometimes helps to place your hand on your belly or chest to feel the rise and fall.
4. Continue for three minutes and notice how you are feeling as the process continues.

You can do this with eyes open or closed; however, I find it more impactful when I close my eyes.

I find that when I meditate often, for small amounts of time, I have greater awareness of when I'm out of balance at work, and have therefore acquired greater skill in learning what I need to do to rebalance. It's like riding a bike. The way you keep a bike balanced is with a lot of micro-recoveries – tilt a little to the left, a little to the right, adjusting slightly to keep balanced.

3. Bum-on-cushion meditation

Meditation is not something you do or achieve. Falling into meditation is like falling asleep: you set up the right conditions for it (by getting yourself ready and comfortable), but you can't make it happen – rather, it's something that just occurs. So, the technique is to simply pay attention to the experience you're having, and to listen as though you're waiting to hear a message.

Here are some steps to guide you if you choose to sit upright and meditate for a longer period of time – say, 20 minutes in the morning or before you go to bed at night. These have been influenced by the teachings of Erich Schiffmann and Richard Miller, great yoga practitioners who taught my yoga teacher Chris Wilson. This is just one pathway for meditation:

1. Begin each sitting period by welcoming yourself home, as if greeting a dear friend.

2. Get the alignment of your body just right. Do you feel balanced, relaxed and really comfortable? Take your time to set this up.

3. Welcome any thoughts, feelings or emotions and welcome their changing nature or movement: simply watch them. Ask yourself, 'How am I?' then wait to feel the answer.

4. Affirm your heartfelt intention for the meditation. Don't overcomplicate this, just listen.

5. Welcome the physical experience (body sensations, sounds and visual experiences).

6. Practise being still without holding yourself still – relax.

7. Notice the movement of breath and ripple of feeling in the body.

8. Notice a felt sense of being that is present amid the experience – the 'observer' self.

9. Enquire into how, by 'allowing' all movement to be fully experienced, this occurs within your awareness. You're just watching, allowing: you're in an experiencing state, rather than a thinking state.

10. Stay open to that awareness.

With a meditation practice, you can continually return the mind to a state of calmness and stillness during any storm that arises. You'll face challenges at work with colleagues and customers with more focus, clarity and energy.

Meditation helps you be more effective as you release your addiction to a scattered mind.

Service Habit 5
MEDITATE DAILY

Reflect now

- How do you get into the moment and give your full attention and concentration?

- How do you achieve a centred feeling?

- Where are you most likely to practise meditation: at home or at work?

- Which of the three styles set out in this chapter would best suit you to begin with?

Embed the habit

Practise any of the three styles of meditation in this chapter to get started on your mental training regime. Start small – you wouldn't go to the gym five days a week for an hour a day if you were just getting started! Set a realistic goal like, say, ten minutes a night, and commit to it.

MY 66-DAY MEDITATION CHALLENGE

If you'd like some extra help, I've created a special suite of 66 unique guided meditations just for you. Go to the link below to access my FREE 66-day meditation challenge.

jaquiescammell.com/66-days-of-meditation

Each meditation is no more than ten minutes – with a different theme, with music and without. By committing to the 66 days of meditation, you are on your way to creating a daily habit that will stick. Let go of any expectations; just be light and play with it.

Service Habit 6
BE THE CHANGE

There's a story about a woman in India who was upset that her son was eating too much sugar. Her concern led her to take her son to see his great hero, Mahatma Gandhi. She approached the great leader, and said, 'Sir, my son eats too much sugar, and it's not good for his health. Would you please tell him to stop?'

Gandhi turned to her son and said, 'Go home and come back in two weeks.' The woman was confused – why hadn't he asked the boy to stop eating sugar? Without a word, though, she took her son's hand and they went home. Two weeks later, they returned, and Gandhi looked directly at the boy and told him, 'You should stop eating sugar. It isn't good for your health.' The boy promised he would give it up.

His mother asked, 'Sir, why didn't you tell him that two weeks ago?' Gandhi smiled, let out a cheeky laugh and said, 'Well, because two weeks ago I was still eating sugar myself.' He would not give advice to anyone that he wasn't willing to role-model himself.

We must model the behaviours we want others to adopt. As Gandhi said: 'If we could change ourselves, the tendencies in the world would also change. As a man changes his own nature, so does the attitude of the world change towards him.'

Or, to paraphrase:

> *Be the change you want to see in the world.*

SERVICE IS A FEELING

I can always tell in the first few minutes of an interaction with an employee whether they're task-oriented or behaviour-oriented. Being served by someone who's simply completing a task can feel shallow, incomplete and transactional – there's little connection to them as a human being. By contrast, when you're served by someone who's mindful of how they're behaving in the interaction, there's more meaning in the exchange. This results in you, the customer, feeling more connected to the brand, the place and the person who served you.

In September 2013, the *American Express Service Study* revealed that of 1620 customers tested, 63 per cent felt their heart rate increase when they thought about receiving great customer service. Another 53 per cent found that receiving great customer service triggered the same cerebral reactions as feeling loved. The takeaway? When it comes to service, it's not just about what your customers think. Great service is about their feelings.

Carl W. Buehner said it well: 'They may forget what you said, but they will never forget how you made them feel.'

A few years back, I interviewed Linda, head of nursing for a private hospital group. She oversaw 150 nurses and had been in the industry for 20 years at that time. She shared with me a process that the organisation had rolled out called 'Random Acts of Kindness', to remind nurses about the basics of talking to patients and to get them to think about performing kind acts. The program was introduced because, even though the nurses thought they were being professional and doing their best, patients felt the opposite.

People defined 'random acts of kindness' as things like smiling, asking about a family member, delivering an extra cup of tea to a patient or ensuring that they had an ice pack if they needed one. When I probed Linda as to why the basic behaviours of kindness needed to be encouraged via a formal process, she explained:

> 'Even in a role like nursing, kindness gets lost in the other stuff. We forget to be human, and we bring our troubles to work, our rushing and busyness to work… we forget to be present to our patients.'

Initially, the program was met with resistance; but, over time, performing random acts of kindness became an embedded habit in the hospitals. Linda observed that the power of the process was in seeing the impact on the patients firsthand – how the small things were actually what made their day. The hospitals' culture, morale and overall patient satisfaction all improved, and the weekly letter from the general manager has a regular feature highlighting patient feedback on the kindness of the hospital staff.

In the best service cultures I have seen, teams understand the expected behaviours in service interactions, and the leaders role-model these expected behaviours each day. At an organisational level, values and behaviours are specific, measurable ways of defining what great service is in your team, so you can recognise them when they are being role-modelled. According to corporate anthropologist Michael Henderson, when you're part of a team with clearly defined values and behaviours, this helps you:

· define what's worth striving for
· define what to say yes and no to
· generate energy and motivation.

Without clearly defined values and behaviours, there will be:

- no clear boundaries or expectations of what good service looks like in teams
- inconsistency of behaviour, and therefore inconsistency of service.

YOU ARE THE COMPANY

It only takes one person in the team to have a bad day to leave a bad impression on customers – like it or not, how a customer feels about their one interaction with one individual is how they feel about the company itself. In other words, in your customers' way of thinking, you are the company.

I'm certain your job description spells out the technical and task-related elements of your role, but your organisation may or may not have well-defined and highly visible values and behaviours. Regardless, you can lead by example, behaving in a way that drives human connection.

How you make people feel comes from who you are being and what you are role-modelling, regardless of the outcome. Sometimes they don't get the outcome that they're looking for, but it's the feeling that the person walks away with that leaves the lasting impression. A customer might feel, for example, 'I didn't get the full refund, but I felt valued and cared for in the way that person handled it, and they gave me the most compensation they could.'

Many of us have had training and years of experience in our jobs, yet it's not solely our technical capability that defines our best professional self.

What you do at work counts, but who you are and how that's experienced by others counts twice as much.

ROLE-MODELLING BEHAVIOURS

The way to tap into people's feelings is by becoming acutely aware of your behaviours.

As we saw with the nurses instructed to perform random acts of kindness, their perception of their behaviour towards their patients was skewed. It wasn't until they paid attention to patients' feedback that they realised their perception was not their patients' experience.

Making decisions throughout the day through the filter of values and behaviours, not solely facts and tasks, is a skill everyone is capable of learning. The choice is yours: you can choose to behave in a way that is meaningful and impactful, and you don't need a company charter to do it if you really want to serve others.

Henderson explains, in his book *Above the Line*:

> *'Your personal values… inform the reticular activated system in your brain, which maintains consciousness and acts as a filter, which in turn enables us to concentrate on what is most important to us and ignore everything else… People with values that are aligned with the work they do are more focused and productive, and more emotionally and mentally rewarded by their work.'*

Every moment matters in service: who you're being, the choices you make and how you behave.

Your behaviours are your values in action

In a professional setting, defining behaviours for each of the company values is often the missing link in creating a great service culture. It is one thing to know the desired values we wish to role-model, but it's another thing to understand what those values look like in action.

One of the easiest ways to address inconsistency with customer service, as I indicated earlier, is to ensure that everyone on the team and in the business is clear about the behaviours expected when interacting with others. When behaviours are explicit, people know what 'good' looks like and have a better chance of high performance.

When you know what 'good behaviour' looks like, you tend to notice it more often and, as explained above, the reticular activated system will go on a fact-finding mission to look for those who continue to demonstrate the ideal behaviours. The perfect formula to fuel a high-performing service team is to:

- be clear on what the ideal behaviours are
- be on the lookout for these ideal behaviours.

When everyone is role-modelling the behaviours, it reinforces what 'good' looks like.

It's the same in a personal setting: your day-to-day behaviours, even in the most ordinary of circumstances, show people loud and clear what you value and what you stand for. For example, imagine you're driving in traffic and you make the decision in a fleeting moment to let another driver in front of you. When you let them in, do you wait for them to give you a little wave of thanks, or are you happy to let them in regardless of whether they thank you or not?

If you are someone who truly values kindness, rather than serving from a place of obligation – which is, of course, fraught with expectations – your act of letting someone in is genuine, regardless of what response you receive. As Wayne W. Dyer said in his book *Everyday Wisdom for Success*, 'Anonymously perform acts of kindness, expecting nothing in return, not even a thank you.'

So, what's most important to you?

- Do you leave people better than you found them?
- Do people gush about your care and kindness?
- Are you leaving an impression on people that makes a difference to their day?

   In service, at work and in life, you bring your purpose and values to life through your actions.

Service Habit 6
BE THE CHANGE

Reflect now

- What are your company's values, and how does the company recommend these be expressed through staff behaviours?
- If the company values are not clearly defined, what are your personal values and how easily are you able to live your personal values at work?
- How often do you apply them, and what indicates to you that you're doing so?
- Who demonstrates these values and behaviours well, in your eyes? Why?
- How can you help other staff members learn these actions?

Embed the habit

Do a self-assessment of your own day-to-day behaviours using a traffic light system:

- Green-light behaviours are those you want to start doing more of, as you know they'll make for better relationships and service.
- Amber-light behaviours are those you're already doing and want to continue in your day-to-day interactions.
- Red-light behaviours are those you want to stop.

You can take this exercise one step further and invite some of your colleagues to do the same activity, and compare notes at the end. If this isn't an activity you're comfortable with, perhaps you can role-model by asking someone in your team, or a peer in another area of the business, to keep you accountable to your green-, amber- and red-light behaviours. You never know – that conversation may inspire them to do the same activity.

Service Habit 7
LOOK THE PART

I've been committed to preparing for first impressions all my working life – influenced by training from great leaders, great organisations and the people who raised me.

From the age of fourteen years and nine months, I was institutionalised into the McDonald's workplace culture, which had the highest grooming, uniform and personal-hygiene standards among fast-food restaurants. I remember worrying about my uniform being crushed if I had an after-school shift, and coming up with creative ways to fold and pack my pressed shirt and trousers to avoid creases.

You would always allow fifteen minutes before your shift to get dressed and prepared. The crew room was the final stop, where the manager would check your appearance from head to toe, ensuring you looked the part. Hair had to be pulled back neat and tidy, minimum jewellery worn, uniform tucked in and presented well, name badge straight and shoes polished and clean. If you got past this checkpoint, you would move through the back-of-house areas towards the front service areas, where you'd be met by a sign that said: 'Smile, you are about to go on stage.' It was reinforced time and time again: when you were within eyesight of a customer, you had to look the part.

I'd experienced the military approach to uniforms and grooming well before my after-school shifts at McDonald's, though. You see, my dad believed that big wins begin with small disciplines and that how you present yourself to the world determines your results. As a result, my brothers and I always had the most highly polished shoes at school. Every Sunday night, we would have to line up in the lounge room and stand on newspaper, with our school shoes in one hand and the polish in the other. This wasn't fancy black polish in a tube that you wiped on, let dry and hey presto! No, we had to polish shoes first with dubbin, then with polish, and then give them a good brush to really bring out the shine. It was a process that Dad wanted to embed in our minds.

Each weekday morning, we woke to the sound of marching music intended to motivate us to get ready, eat breakfast and get to school. In the evenings, we followed a strict routine of making lunches, packing schoolbags, finishing homework and going to bed early – all planned to the minute. These small disciplines – tiny habits – were Dad's way of reinforcing how important it was to look the part and be prepared.

In my adult life, I still believe that how you present yourself to others sets the tone. It plays a tangible role in making your service to others memorable and satisfying. Looking the part is not about being vain: rather, it's about giving your first interaction with a customer or colleague the best start and getting into a frame of mind that makes you feel ready to serve.

Before you can deliver exceptional service, you have to prepare and practise the little things. Look the part to feel the part.

FIRST IMPRESSIONS COUNT

'You never get a second chance to make a first impression,' goes the adage. According to leading social psychologist Mark Schaller in his chapter of the book *First Impressions*, we make a first impression within seven seconds.

In a few seconds, without you even speaking, the perception you create says volumes to people. For example:

· A 2011 study by Tilburg University in the Netherlands found that people wearing name-brand clothes – such as Lacoste and Tommy Hilfiger – during a first impression were perceived as having higher status than folks wearing non-designer clothes.

· A 2012 University of Pennsylvania study found that men with shaved heads were rated as more dominant than similar men with full heads of hair, as a first impression.

So, regardless of your role, your industry, your age or your experience, you must consider first impressions. There are five areas in which it's critical that you make a good first impression when you're serving others:

1. appearance
2. posture and eye contact
3. smile
4. gestures
5. language.

Let's look at each of these in turn.

Appearance

The way you present yourself is the first thing to get right when you work in a professional service environment. Your grooming – hair, fingernails, clothing, make-up and facial hair – sends a strong message to people, and it also has an impact on how you feel while working there. For the customer and for yourself, you want that nonverbal message to be positive.

When you walk into a room, your energy introduces you before you speak. Putting on your uniform, for example, or dressing to serve, can signal an energy state change within you. It can be a trigger to set your mindset to 'I'm ready to serve'. What you wear and your physical preparedness in your appearance impacts the way you feel at work, which in turn has an impact on how people feel towards you.

The great work-from-home experiment created by the COVID-19 pandemic has tested this theory and pushed the boundaries of people dressing for work – or not – while working from home. We see professionals who typically made an effort to dress for their workplace's office environment now attending work meetings (via Zoom or Microsoft Teams) dressed in their activewear. What does this appearance do for their mindset and their readiness to serve? How does it influence the experience of people who are viewing them on screen?

Posture and eye contact

A straight posture signals confidence, so stand tall when you greet people for the first time.

In service, it's about creating confidence. When you and your team move between interactions and moments throughout a day, you want to make each customer or colleague you are interacting with feel confident about their relationship with you. If your posture is signalling doubt, tiredness or boredom, for example, you are giving the other person a reason to be less confident about the relationship. You want your posture and body language to give the impression that they are in safe hands and you have the ability to solve their problems.

You've probably been told at some point that making eye contact is a signal of sincerity. Did you know that, according to the research, it also makes you seem smarter? 'People who make more eye contact are perceived as more intelligent', reported the British Psychological Society in its *Research Digest* blog, regarding a study conducted at the University of Michigan. By contrast, 'people who avoid eye contact are judged to be insincere and lacking in conscientiousness.'

In a world where, as I write, we're leaving our homes with a face mask as a mandatory accessory, making eye contact in service has become even more critical to making positive first impressions and gaining trust.

Smile

An ancient Chinese proverb has it that, 'A man without a smiling face must not open a shop.' Surely a smile is a prerequisite for anyone in business when they're serving humans? Yet we see so many people metaphorically 'opening their shops' with few or no smiles on their faces.

Smiling can actually boost your immune system and your physical health as well as your happiness, allowing you to live up to seven years longer! If you struggle to keep smiling all day, remember:

· Happiness is more contagious than sadness, so surround yourself with happy, smiling people.

· Imitate happy, positive people; do what they do.

You have the power to bring more joy into your own life and into the lives of others – by smiling more.

To help others smile more, try these tactics:

· Smile first yourself. Give them one of your smiles – they're free!

· Show some interest by asking a question that will lead to a conversation – hopefully, a conversation that gets them smiling.

Gestures

A few simple gestures will help you make a great first impression. Keep your arms relaxed and by your side to show you're open to what others are communicating, and when you speak, use your hands – this improves your credibility with the listener. Lean in to show interest and tilt your head slightly when you're being spoken to, to show you're listening. If you're in an environment where first meetings generally involve a handshake, make sure your handshake is firm but not too firm. If a handshake is not appropriate, then a simple nod of the head in acknowledgement of the person can still make for a great first impression.

In a world where people are encouraged to socially distance and keep 1.5 metres apart, and facial gestures are sometimes not easily visible behind masks, hand gestures, leaning in and use of arms have become more critical in communicating.

Language

Speak clearly, with an even tone: you don't want to be too loud or too quiet. Make sure your voice conveys confidence and credibility. A steady voice, using a steady breath, will give greater confidence when speaking. When someone is breathy and their voice a little shaky, it creates a sense of doubt and uncertainty. Be sure to adjust your language to suit the situation, whether that's speaking to a colleague using professional jargon or using every-day terms and avoiding acronyms with a customer. Always use non-offensive language.

Using fewer, carefully chosen words often creates a lasting, strong first impression. When you speak using too many words, your key message can get lost. You want to use language to catch people's attention, be memorable and build trust with them.

You may be able to engage a colleague or customer immediately by starting with a statement like, 'I'm really impressed by the way you…' or 'I love the shoes you're wearing.' Starting with a compliment is always a winner – if it's genuine, of course.

TRUST ME

In her book *Presence*, Amy Cuddy (a Harvard psychologist who has spent 15 years studying first impressions) states that people answer two basic questions during a first impression that determine whether they like you and want to conduct business with you. These two questions are:

1. Can I trust this person?
2. Can I respect this person?

Trustworthiness is referred to as 'warmth' by psychologists; warmth is about making the other person feel understood. Respect is referred to as 'competence'. Importantly, even though competence in a work environment is highly valued, it's only evaluated *after* trust is established. In other words:

Trust trumps your level of skill in a role.

This means that mastering your first impression on others may set you apart, even when other people are more competent or qualified than you are.

Think about what you look for, in those first few seconds, when you're a customer. What judgements do you make that instantly lead you to a decision about whether you trust or respect the other person? Here are some of mine:

· If I arrive at a cafe or restaurant and the front dining area is untidy and dirty, I conclude that the food handling out the back is of a poor standard.

· If I walk up to a reception area and am greeted by an employee who has grubby hands and a poorly presented uniform, I conclude they'll be careless with my needs.

- If I jump into the back of an Uber or taxi and the driver is warm, friendly and greets me with positive energy, I conclude that I'm in good hands and am confident they'll get me to my destination safely.

Job interviews are another obvious situation in which you have to make a good first impression. If you do an online search for the term 'job interview', you'll be bombarded with countless publications and articles that say this.

However, also think about the less obvious moments in a working day when you're trying to build trust and respect with those around you. For example, some of my clients work in large airports, shopping precincts, venues and stadiums. They have a long way to travel within their workplace before they get to their workstations or 'clock on' for their shift. I encourage them to think about the impression they give off when they're walking through the staff car park, catching the staff shuttle bus, walking through security or grabbing a coffee at the staff cafe. These are all touchpoints at which people will form impressions based on the way you interact with them.

A wise mentor of mine reminds me often, 'You are always being interviewed.' What he's saying is that people never stop forming opinions of you: whether you're looking for work or not, looking to impress someone or not, the way you interact with people when you first meet them leaves an imprint in their mind. So much so that it could lead, one day, to someone handing you a business card and offering you a job out of the blue!

Pause for a moment and take a snapshot of yourself. If someone were to approach you right now to meet you for the first time, what impression would you make on them in those first few crucial seconds?

People are always watching. People experience you moment to moment, and at the end of the day, the customer chooses what they think of you and the business you work for based on the quality of the impressions you've made in any given moment.

SHOW UP

Part of your role in delivering service is to show up and be fully present with the people you serve. To be able to do this, you need to put some fundamentals in place before you arrive at work. It starts before you leave home:

- What's your energy like when you're getting ready to go to work? Are you feeling positive about the day ahead or dreading the next eight hours?
- Have you allowed yourself time to eat and to present yourself cleanly?
- Have you allowed enough time to get to work, instead of madly rushing and starting your day in a panic?

One of my own weekly disciplines is to prepare myself on Sunday for the week ahead. I sit down with my calendar open and look at the client meetings and customer workshops I've scheduled. I think about the conversations I'll be having and my level of preparedness for them. I look at how much yoga I've scheduled in to keep my body and mind balanced, and how much time I've allowed for critical thinking and reflection. While this may seem overly structured, it sets me up to feel, 'I'm ready and I'm intentional about the impact I want to have on others!'

What about you: what do you do to prepare yourself and give yourself the best chance to show up at your best?

Make it a habit to show up as your best professional self.

PRACTISE MAINTAINING A POSITIVE MINDSET

You will undoubtedly face problems in a service role. You'll be dealing with customers who could be anything from happy to mildly annoyed to outright angry; anyone who's spent time in a customer-focused role will have experienced the full range of emotions! The key to overcoming problems is to put yourself in a positive mindset before you arrive at work. This way, you have a better chance of behaving with grace and gratitude.

You can be grateful that your customers are approaching you with their problems: it gives you an opportunity to add value to their experience by resolving their issues.

So, as you get ready, or when you're making your way into work, think about the kind of people you want to meet and the kind of interactions you want to have. This can be incredibly grounding and works very well to focus you on the kind of energy you want to have for your day.

DO THE PRE-WORK

Whether you're a frontline employee serving customers all day or a leader serving a team, you need to be knowledgeable in your job role. For frontline employees, many organisations provide well-planned training calendars to help them meet ever-changing standards for compliance and product knowledge. Leaders often need to do a great deal of independent preparation:

· reading or writing reports
· critical thinking on matters of strategy and performance
· having specific conversations to gather evidence, context and points of view
· analysing relevant data to inform a decision.

However, not all pre-work can be done on the job. Homework doesn't end when you leave school, if you want to be well prepared and make a good first impression. For example:

- If you'll be meeting a client or customer for the first time, who are they? What questions can you ask them to gain necessary information?

- If you're meeting the team to discuss an issue around their service interactions, what are some examples you can refer to? Who else shares the same views? What questions can you start the meeting with to gain necessary information?

Pre-work could involve researching a topic or issue, or crafting several questions that get a conversation off to a great start – anything that will make for a productive interaction, which will, in turn, deepen your relationships.

Those who are committed to serving people put time aside to think and prepare before they meet them.

LOOK THE PART

Reflect now

- What would it feel like to be on the receiving end of your first impression?

- What are some examples of possible poor first impressions at your work? What would be the cost of them?

- What factors contribute towards a good or poor first impression in your work environment?

- What do you need to do in the morning or at the beginning of your week to prepare your mindset?

- What little things do you need to do to keep your self-awareness sharp when making a first impression?

Embed the habit

Sometimes, it's easier to observe these things in others before we turn attention to ourselves:

- Make a list of the first impressions you look for when you interact with others.

- Flip that list and be your own critic. How are others responding to you? Do you get a sense that trust and respect are being created during your first impression?

- Approach someone you trust – a friend or colleague – and ask them to answer these two questions honestly:

    1. If you were meeting me for the first time today, what does my appearance tell you?

    2. What other factors create my first impression?

Pillar 2
UNDERSTAND OTHERS

THIS SECOND PILLAR is where we start to refine skills in using good judgement in service situations that are critical to relationships. If the ultimate goal in customer service is to strengthen relationships and create trust and loyalty, then good judgement comes through the practice of empathy.

The next seven service habits give you practical ways to make people feel seen, heard and understood, so that you can provide the appropriate solutions and create greater connections.

When you're finished reading about these seven habits, you will:

·   see how to be more connected with the people you serve

·   see people's perspectives more clearly

·   fine-tune your listening to the next level

·   craft your questions for better conversations.

You will also become a master at remembering people's names!

Service Habit 8
PUT THE TEAM FIRST

In 2019, one of Australia's leading airlines invited me to come and observe their operations behind the scenes at their head office in Sydney. However, my arrival coincided with the 2019 Hong Kong protests – known as the Anti-Extradition Law Amendment Bill Movement – which were an ongoing series of demonstrations. The crisis had grounded many airlines and passengers, which created a great deal of work and activity for multiple teams involved in taking care of customers' safety and getting them to their destinations.

Walking through the restricted areas of their head office, I observed engineers, meteorologists, coordinators of crew and customer care teams all working harmoniously together to deal with a problem that was out of their control yet was impacting their customers greatly. I witnessed professionalism, orderly discussions and meetings taking place: people were having calm and respectful conversations with each other as the day presented multiple challenges by the minute.

There were little gems of service sprinkled throughout the floor:

- employees serving an unprompted mug of coffee to a colleague who hadn't been home for 24 hours

- a conversation I overheard at a water cooler between two ladies, in which one lady offered to pick up the other's children from school so that she could stay focused on the complaints

- the guy in the control centre suggesting he could stay back a few more hours to oversee the screens, to allow his colleague to go shower and have some lunch.

This was no act on the part of the staff members, no façade to make customers happy: this was who they were behind the scenes during a time of great pressure and uncertainty. As a customer of this airline, to witness the culture of the organisation during a time of crisis gave me great confidence in flying with them.

You can tell a lot about an organisation by the way its employees treat each other.

There is a certain mimicry that takes place in a workplace. Employees' behavioural traits rub off onto each other and combine to prescribe how people act around the workplace. It takes a huge amount of effort to then change these behavioural traits when you're in front of a customer.

What you do as a culture, a workforce, when no-one is watching is your true nature in service. The level of service given to people outside of the organisation – customers and suppliers, for example – should take little effort, but if service teams are having to make extra effort because it's not their 'natural' approach to internal relationships, they will soon start to tire.

Have you ever walked into a bank branch and overheard two employees gossiping about their manager before they realise that you're there waiting to be served? How would this experience influence your confidence in the employees, and how would you feel about having them take care of your important financial affairs?

Have you ever been in a queue in a supermarket and heard the employee behind the counter being reprimanded by a manager for making a mistake? How would this experience influence your impression of how genuine the manager's care and concern for you is, now that you've witnessed them giving their own employee a dressing-down in front of you?

The best customer-service cultures are a direct reflection of their working culture, because this is effortless and how people naturally behave. You have a much better chance of providing consistent service if you serve people inside and outside in the same way.

> *How you treat your colleagues is a reflection of how you treat customers.*

THE CUSTOMER DOESN'T ALWAYS COME FIRST

As a service leader or service professional, you know how important it is to deliver great results to a customer – you've been encouraged to put the customer first. You've been conditioned to believe that all your efforts need to be in service of your customers' needs. The consequence, in many workplaces, is that people like you neglect the needs of their colleagues. Before you look externally towards your customers, you must first look internally at how you treat each of your colleagues.

On the whole, in today's workplace environments, leaders:

- overcommit with busy schedules
- bounce between back-to-back meetings
- leave very little time for building relationships with their team members.

In addition, frontline employees:

- limit their efforts to the work that only impacts them

- bounce between tasks and miss opportunities to be helpful to their teammates
- leave very little time for teamwork, collaboration and good-spirited support.

The team must come first.

How are people behaving? How do staff treat each other throughout the day? How do staff cope with challenges, high-pressure moments and giving each other feedback? Do staff understand each other's needs and empathise with their co-workers? There's no point focusing on the quality of your service externally if the service among your teams and across departments is not a genuine, healthy reflection of what you desire to project towards your customers.

When you're delivering service externally that is incongruent with how you serve each other internally, your service performance will be inconsistent and insincere, and it will come unstuck in the times that matter the most. Furthermore, if you only dial up your treatment and care towards people externally and neglect the relationships internally, you run the risk of:

- having to apply more effort to serve customers, because this is not your natural behaviour
- delivering shallow and transactional service to the customer, because this is your natural behaviour behind the scenes
- having inconsistent customer-service levels across the workforce, because there is no standard or practice internally that is ingrained in the DNA of the team.

Why should it be any different externally? It would be like keeping the front porch of your house clean and tidy to make a good impression on the neighbours and passers-by, yet when you invite people inside for a cup of tea, they find that the place is dirty, untidy and chaotic – not at all a reflection of the outside.

How long can you keep up a façade of who you want to be with customers, when inside the house is not in order?

There's a saying, 'Service is a performance', and there is an element of truth to that, but isn't it easier if how we are during service is how we are everywhere, with everyone? It's more effort to be someone we're not than it is to be the same everywhere – to be of service everywhere.

> The level of effort you put into keeping a brand, reputation and service of a high quality is also required internally in your workplace.

CUSTOMERS' EXPERIENCES REFLECT EMPLOYEES' EXPERIENCES

There's a direct correlation between employee experience and customer experience when it comes to a business's profitability. Talent organisation Accenture reported in 2017 that 51 per cent of the business leaders surveyed plan their employee experiences, knowing this will impact the customer experience.

It's crucial to maintain healthy workplace relationships. You project onto your colleagues what you are feeling on the inside, and they do the same. If you're confused inside, you'll experience confusion on the outside. If you're happy and content on the inside, you'll experience happiness and contentment on the outside. So, it makes sense to take really good care of each other at work – in fact, it more than makes sense! You must be conscious of what you're reflecting to your team, as it will impact the way your colleagues feel and therefore the way they perform at work.

How your employees are together – their small talk, response times, language and behaviour – that is their true service culture and that is what will be mirrored to customers, whether you like it or not.

The quality of your relationships with your customers reflects the quality of your relationships with your colleagues.

Over a decade ago, I was running the food and beverage contract for a large venue during a stressful period when we were being assessed on whether our contract would be renewed. When I began leading the team, they had a silo mentality – meaning, they all just did their own thing in their department or area of work without really understanding the impact their work had on others. There was certainly not a level of service to be proud of among the teams; nothing of a standard that would be considered suitable for a paying customer.

I found it strange that the teams went to so much effort to take great care of the paying customer, but when it came to taking care of each other – the people they served all day at work – there was a less considerate approach.

So, I set them a challenge, which was met with much resistance. I asked all the full-time employees to create a roster assigning them to spend one week in the shoes of a colleague in a completely different department. Chefs had to work in accounts; accounts had to work in stores and delivery. Human resources had to do operations for a week and operations had to do recruitment. We called it 'a week in the life' and it really ruffled people's feathers. Yet the result was profound.

At the end of the week, the teams shared that the experience had been highly valuable, giving them new insight into the overall success of the business. I noticed a shift, with more:

- concern and consideration for processes and how they impacted other departments
- understanding and empathy for other departments when they were having a particularly tough day

- communication across departments
- questions and curiosity across departments about what was working and what was not
- teamwork
- collaboration.

There was a greater appreciation for what individuals did for each other, and a deeper understanding between the teams: people knew what others needed in order to perform at their best in their role. All of a sudden, as a result, people were starting to serve each other – being helpful, addressing problems and removing barriers.

Your colleagues are your internal customers. They deserve your focus, your attention, your commitment and dedication, just as a paying customer does. They want to be heard and understood, and treated with care and kindness, just like a paying customer does. They want to feel that they're a priority and that you're interested in their happiness, just like a paying customer does.

How well do you know your internal customers, and how intentional are you about ensuring that you serve them just as you would a paying customer?

NO AGENDAS

Your colleagues are your internal customers: they, too, deserve your focus and attention. The best way to invest in relationships and serve your internal customers is to get to know them – meaning, to catch up with them with no agenda.

One of my clients who runs an airport shared with me that they've introduced what they call 'Happy chat Fridays'. The manager of the airport has a ten-minute sit-down with each staff member to talk about whatever that person wants to talk about. It's a small amount of time; however, it provides a cadence for ensuring that people are constantly getting to communicate with, relate to and understand each other with no agenda or specific outcome in mind.

You may find that, in your organisation, there are opportunities throughout a day that are less structured but just as impactful.

Ask yourself:

· Does your diary/schedule allow for 'no agenda' time?

· Do you attend some or all of the social events that your organisation hosts?

· Do you get involved in conversations at the water cooler and the coffee machine?

· Do you know where your colleagues live and how they travel to work each day?

· Do you know your colleagues' interests outside of work; where they're taking their next holiday; the football team they support?

· Do you know if they drink tea or coffee, and have you ever offered to get them one?

These are the fundamentals of building rapport, breaking down barriers between people and coming to understand people more deeply. The more you can relate to your colleagues, crack a joke, lighten their day and serve them, the better your team will serve customers. This is not about wasting time or prioritising socialising over getting the job done. It's about approaching each relationship with respect and curiosity, and valuing one another.

When you have quality relationships internally, you'll see a rise in team efficiency and alignment:

· Conversations will flow more easily.

· People will take things less personally and more professionally.

- People will be less interested in individual success and see their value in contributing to the greater success of the business.

Prioritise your relationships internally so you can better serve in your relationships externally.

Here are some of my favourite ways of consciously making no-agenda time to hang out with my colleagues when walking around the office area:

- When I make a coffee in the tearoom, I allow a good ten minutes so I can interact and engage in small talk and banter while waiting for the coffee to filter.
- When I have lunch, I make sure I sit in a common area where I can talk to people and listen to conversations, rather than eating at my desk.
- When I arrive most mornings, I make sure I walk through the office area and say hello to everyone before I get stuck into my work for the day.

As I've said before, investing in internal relationships is no different to serving customers. If a customer appeared within a few metres of you, you would raise your head, make eye contact and smile. If a customer called you and you were with someone else, you'd call them back at your earliest convenience. If a customer asked to see you, you'd make it a priority to see them.

We need to nurture a customer service mindset inside the walls of our workplaces first, in order for the relationships on the outside to thrive.

Service Habit 8
PUT THE TEAM FIRST

Reflect now

- Who are your internal customers?
- What do you do for others at work?
- What do others do for you at work?
- What's the pay-off when you have great relationships at work?
- What do you gain?

Embed the habit

1. Draw a line horizontally across the middle of a blank page, so the page is split into two.

2. In the upper half, reflect on what you do every day in the workplace that has a significant impact on others you work with, and ultimately on their ability to be their best professional selves and deliver excellent customer service. For example, you might process an order that allows a sales representative to deliver on their promise to the customer.

3. Still in the upper half of the page, write a list of the colleagues whose performance you have an impact on each day at work.

4. In the lower half of the page, list the individuals within your organisation who directly or indirectly have an impact on you and your ability to be the best professional you can be.

5. Once your lists are complete, ask yourself these questions:
    - How well do I know these people?
    - How well do they know me?
    - What could I do in the short term to deepen these relationships?
    - What could I do on an ongoing basis to deepen these relationships?

Service Habit 9
USE THEIR NAME

My friend Pete was the CEO of a business school. Every 90 days, the school community would gather for a three-day event; with up to 150 students, 30 faculty and then the team members, there would be over 200 people in a room at once. Yet when any one of the students put their hand up to contribute, Pete would call on them by name. When he saw people in the corridor during the event, he didn't have a sneaky glance at their lanyard: he knew each person's name, even if it was the first time he had met them.

When I asked Pete how he managed to remember all those names every time, he explained that he had made a decision, when he became CEO, to ensure that he knew everyone's name. He said, 'People have invested their money, their time and their faith in our program. I can show them the respect they deserve by at least knowing each person's name. In the week leading up to the quarterly events, I play a flashcard game on a screen, recognising people's faces and their names, to ensure I've built muscle around each person's name.'

This was a CEO who valued his time immensely, but still felt it was worth sitting down and learning people's names. Like anything, it takes practice.

Remembering their names is the first courtesy we extend to people we serve.

WHAT'S IN A NAME?

Think about your own name for a moment:

· Is there a story behind your name?

· Are you named after a family member or someone famous?

· Do you have a nickname or a middle name?

· Do you like your name? Why or why not?

· In what ways (if any) do you identify with your name?

Our identity is wrapped up in our name. So, when someone we don't know (or don't know very well) calls us by our name, we feel recognised, it makes us feel good and it immediately creates rapport. In his book *How to Win Friends and Influence People*, Dale Carnegie put it, 'Remember that a person's name is, to that person, the sweetest and most important sound in any language.'

If you've ever visited the stores of Nike, lululemon or Apple, then a staff member likely asked you your name. This is an official part of their greeting process; I have even witnessed, on numerous occasions at lululemon, my name being written on the change room door. This simple step in their processes personalises the service and makes customers feel special.

Using people's names is particularly beneficial when a conversation goes badly. Having to confront someone about an issue or deliver some bad news is challenging at the best of times. As soon as the other person sees the conversation deteriorating, they're likely to start to get stuck in their head, overthink the situation and maybe even plan their response. When you say the other person's name, you grab their attention; it can be an effective way to bring them back to the conversation. Subtle use of an individual's name also gives them a level of confidence that, 'Even if you're not the right person to help me, I trust that you'll find someone who can help me.'

When you use someone's name, you can use the formal or informal version. My formal name, for example, is 'Ms Scammell', and using it can be a sign of respect; however, watch for people's reaction, as use of the formal name can sometimes have an adverse effect. The informal version of my name is 'Jaqs' – this is more casual. Again, though, watch for people's reaction, as using an informal name may appear too casual and friendly – it's best to ask for permission first.

Some organisations have a standard approach to using customers' names. However, I like to follow the rule of thumb of mirroring how the person introduces themselves to you. If they introduce themselves as 'Ms Brown' or 'Mr Lee', then that's how they want you to address them. You can also simply ask what they prefer to be called.

Beware of overusing people's names in service, though. If you use someone's name too much, you may appear to be trying to manipulate them, and this is likely to do the reverse of building rapport.

PAY ATTENTION

Some people have an uncanny ability for remembering people's names. One of the most common things I hear in group sessions, however, is, 'I'm not good at remembering people's names.' The good news is that it's an easy skill to acquire. To get better at remembering names, all you have to do is pay attention.

Just as we discussed in Service Habit #4, 'Watch your thoughts'. When you're introduced to someone for the first time, what are you thinking? Chances are, the more present you are when you meet someone, the better you'll remember their name.

Remembering people's names is not a memory challenge – it's an attention challenge.

Here are six steps to remembering people's names at work and when you're serving others:

1. *Change your belief.* The thought that you're no good at names is unhelpful and limits your commitment to learning. Think about learning names like learning another language. To learn another language, you have to commit to it. It's easier to revert to speaking English, but that's lazy and won't help you gain respect and trust if you're in a non-English-speaking country. The same applies with names: you have to make an effort to remember people's names, gain their trust and show them that you're committed to remembering.

2. *Focus your attention.* Forgetting people's names isn't a memory problem – it's a focus problem. When you're about to enter an environment where you need to use people's names, pay attention. Take some deep breaths, clear your mind of unrelated thoughts and focus on the person when they tell you their name. Commit to being present in that moment.

3. *Repeat or write their name.* In the first five to ten seconds of meeting someone, repeat their name out loud: 'Hi John, nice to meet you.' Try to say their name three times in the first few minutes to anchor the name in your memory. Write the name down if you're in a meeting, or put in on the receipt if it's a customer.

4. *Clarify the spelling.* When you hear someone's name, ask for clarification on the spelling. For example, is it 'Sarah' or 'Sara'? If the name is unusual, you can also offer a compliment and ask about its origin.

5. *Associate something with the name.* Link the person's name to a celebrity or use memorable alliteration, like 'Ben from Bendigo'. So as not to appear derogatory, do this in your mind and don't share the association out loud.

6. *Use your own name when speaking.* Introduce yourself, no matter how brief the interaction may be. Your name will immediately personalise the experience and transform it from a transaction to a meaningful interaction. I'm also a huge fan of people in service roles using name tags or identification lanyards, as these give the customer permission to use your name and help them remember it.

From the early years of school right through to today, people who have used my name and remembered me have had a larger influence on me. That lesson has stuck with me: using a person's name is one of the fastest ways to show them they're important to you.

Learning their name and using it makes people feel seen, heard and important.

USE THEIR NAME

Reflect now

- How do you remember people's names when you meet them for the first time?

- How do you feel, as a customer, when you're addressed by name?

- Why do you believe using names is a good practice in service?

Embed the habit

Start practising using names immediately, and don't hesitate to be obvious about it. If people notice, great: it's a conversation point, and you can explain why you're making a concerted effort to use names.

- Never say 'I'm not good at remembering people's names' ever again.

- Practise in meetings: start each meeting with a quick round of introductions to make sure everyone knows everyone else's names.

- Practise on the phone when serving customers or colleagues: repeat their name in the greeting immediately. Don't forget to give your name, too.

- Practise when serving customers face to face. If you have a regular customer, introduce yourself and don't hesitate to use their name immediately.

- Also, do a quick scan of your work environment for any subtle ways to reinforce people's names in your memory, such as name plates at workstations, name badges or lanyards.

Service Habit 10
SEE THEIR WORLD

Have you ever heard of the 'empty chair technique'? It's a well-known customer service approach devised by Jeff Bezos, founder and former CEO of Amazon. His philosophy in business, which was arguably a large contributor to the company's success, is to always consider what the customer might think of their decisions.

In management meetings, Bezos put an empty chair in the middle of the boardroom or meeting room and then asked his team to imagine that one of their customers was sitting in that chair. The chair prompted the team to ensure they captured the voice of their customers in all key decision-making processes: it was an exercise designed to develop empathy. They asked questions such as:

- What would the customer say is their biggest pain point with our brand currently?

- What would the customer think when we put these ideas forward?

- How happy would the customer feel with the decision we have made today?

- How would the customer want to receive this message?

- What else have we not thought about that the customer would raise if they were in the room today?

This helped the leadership team to get into the customer's shoes and see their decision-making from the customer's perspective. It's the quickest way to dial up your understanding of the needs of the people you serve. This exercise need not be limited to the customer, either: it could be adapted to focus on colleagues or staff.

Think about the people you serve each day. How well do you know their problems? Can you see things from their perspective? When people feel that you've genuinely considered them in your actions and behaviours, they're more willing to cooperate with and be influenced by you. If you don't consider the people you serve and aren't curious about what they're experiencing, you're at risk of:

- solving the wrong problems
- misreading their needs
- miscommunicating.

It's easy to get so caught up in the busyness of your role that you forget what you're there to do and who you're there to do it for. Simple tools like the empty chair technique keep you focused on what and who is important. They're great levellers, reminding you that you're in a relationship with the people you serve, whether they're colleagues, customers, suppliers, staff or superiors.

DIFFERENT WORLD VIEWS

The mind and world view of each person you interact with are different. Think of world view as being like a map. Each of us carry different maps, mostly to do with the unconscious interactions between our thoughts and emotions. Our life experiences and the way we were raised and influenced by school, family and community shape how we form concepts and build meaning from our experiences – and eventually lead us to have our own unique views.

Let's say that you and I take a drive together today: you in the passenger seat, me in the driver's seat. We would be in the same vehicle together, travelling on the same road, but your views and experience would be different to mine. I might pay more attention to the street signs and traffic lights. You might tune in more to the trees and houses. Same experience, different view and meaning drawn from that experience.

The key to seeing other people's worlds is to get curious about them, and to remember that everyone's map is different.

SEE ME, HEAR ME, MAKE ME FEEL I MATTER

The ultimate goal in service is to make people feel seen, heard and understood. One word to sum this up is 'empathy'.

Jacinda Ardern, the Prime Minister of New Zealand as I write this, was very quickly shown to be a leader who demonstrates empathy after the March 2019 terrorist attacks in Christchurch. In her response to the Muslim community, she wore a hijab, the head covering worn by some Muslim women, and her expression was one of concern. Her words, 'They are us', indicated equality and openness. This was not a political speech; this was a human simply listening to other humans and showing them that they were seen, heard and important. This was an indication that she was trying to understand what it might be like to be a member of the Muslim community at that time.

In order for you to satisfy people's needs and be helpful, you need to see the world through their eyes. This is empathy. It's showing people that you see them: all of them. (Did you know that the Zulu people of Africa often use the greeting 'Sawubona', which means, 'I see you'?)

SERVICE IS UNDERSTANDING

The great news is that our brains are wired to be understanding, and when we pay attention to others and try to understand their experience, we can be very effective in relationships. As Daniel Goleman, science journalist and author of the bestselling book *Emotional Intelligence*, co-wrote in the *Harvard Business Review* article 'Social intelligence and the biology of leadership', 'The salient discovery is that certain things leaders do – specifically, exhibit empathy and become attuned to others' moods – literally affect both their own brain chemistry and that of their followers.'

This doesn't just apply to leaders, of course. According to neuroscientists, it seems that 'mirror neurons' in our brains are linked to empathy. Essentially, when we observe an emotion, sensation or behaviour in someone else, these mirror neurons mimic it so that we have a (faint) echo of the experience. This helps us to feel what other people are feeling, not just understand what they're thinking.

Why did the brain evolve this amazing network loop? Some scientists say it was for protection: so that we can observe when others are hurt and avoid being hurt in the same way ourselves. Others say we're wired this way to motivate us to help others, as this creates direct benefits for the family, community, society and the whole of humankind.

When your mirror neurons are firing on all cylinders in a service environment, you see:

· fewer misunderstandings

· quicker problem-solving

· greater emotional connection

· deeper relationships.

When you start to tune into what people may be feeling, you can have a greater impact on those you help and serve.

However, you need to observe and be present in order to fire up your mirror neurons.

EMPATHY IS A PROCESS, NOT AN OUTCOME

Empathy is not an outcome, it's a process: it's understanding others. You don't need to agree with the other person's opinion or see things in the same way, but you can try to understand their views during a particular interaction.

We don't always see eye to eye with other people. I see this often in the group workshops that I facilitate. Someone shares something and others disagree with it, and they may find themselves slipping into a negative or hostile tone. This kind of disagreeing, rebuking and, in some cases, arguing is an essential part of critical thinking. There's a collective genius in a group of people with varied opinions, and such interactions help you develop sound reasoning – more points of view lead to better decision-making! So, I secretly get very excited when people's opinions come to the surface. I always find it fascinating, however, that people forget that you can disagree and still be harmonious.

There's a misconception that service professionals always need to agree with customers. The famous saying bantered around organisations, 'The customer is always right', has led some employees to become people-pleasers even when the customer is wrong. People-pleasing is needed to a point in service, but not at the server's expense. Sometimes, you need to draw the line and present the facts – to find a way to agree to disagree, yet still be liked!

Your goal in service should be to be inclusive: responding to people in a way that reinforces that what they say matters and that you have something more to offer.

One of the reasons I love working and teaching in the service space is that it gives me an opportunity to improve how I approach life. It forces me to embrace everyone's different opinions and standards.

Our job when serving others is to listen to the voice of the larger community, not just our own voice.

Empathy helps us to build relationships despite disagreements, allow others to contribute, and cooperate and act in harmony with them. The key is to be genuine and sincere, and when people feel your level of care and concern for them, they will feel seen, heard and understood.

PRACTISING EMPATHY

What can we do to be more empathic with colleagues and customers in our working day? How can we get into their heads and try to see the world from their point of view? Here are four steps that will help:

1. Be curious.
2. Make eye contact.
3. Ask yourself, 'What's it like to be you?'
4. Use empathy statements.

Be curious

Empathy starts with observation: serving people with curiosity and a watchful eye. Look for any commonalities you may have with someone you're serving, and use these as a quick way of breaking down any barriers. For example, a retail sales assistant might comment on a customer's handbag and mention that she has a similar bag. Perhaps a colleague has a cat or dog, just as you do, and you can connect over the challenges of pet ownership. It doesn't have to be work related: the point is to 'see them' as a human and show that you're interested in learning more about them.

Make eye contact

Have you ever heard the saying, 'The eyes are the windows to the soul'? Lock eyes with someone for a moment and you gain a sense of what they may be feeling or thinking. You can see frustration in someone's eyes – or sadness, excitement or anticipation. In the service industry, it's recommended that you make eye contact at eye level with person you're serving: so, you would crouch down to speak to a small child or someone in a wheelchair.

Ask yourself, 'What's it like to be you?'

When you're interacting with someone, silently ask yourself, 'What's it like to be you?' This immediately helps you imagine their point of view. Ask yourself this question throughout the day, and try using sticky notes to remind you when you're on the phone or crafting emails.

Use empathy statements

Using empathy statements may feel natural for some people; for others, it may require some practice. Either way, it's a skill we all can build to create unique and special responses to our customers.

Following are some empathy statements that you can build on or tailor to suit the unique customer and their needs. The key words are highlighted for you so you can see what makes each one an empathy statement:

- '**I see** that you are surprised by the recent change in our policy.'
- '**I hear** the frustration that you have.'
- '**I understand** your concern and what you need to solve the problem.'

One of the magic words to always try and use in empathy statements is the word 'AND'. The word 'and' is inclusive; it maintains a positive conversation. Whatever your colleague or customer has said or done, you are indirectly offering something more: an alternative or something else for them to consider.

You never want to create a feeling of 'us versus them' or 'I'm right and you're wrong'. Rather, when it comes to serving your teams and your customers, you want them to feel that you're empathising with them, hearing them and understanding their point of view.

This also means that wherever possible, you should try to avoid using the word 'BUT'. Many people approach an opinion or a criticism with some sort of praise or positive comment, followed by the word 'but'. It's a form of manipulation, in a way, in which people give their praise before they reveal their real motive. For example:

> 'I respect your feedback, but we never have issues with
> our products.'

See how it works? The word 'but' ends the dialogue. It says, 'The first truth in this sentence is not nearly as important as the second truth', and the people you speak to will question the sincerity of your initial praise and begin to distrust you.

So, what if you were to switch out the word 'but' for the word 'and'? With the same example, the same message, using 'and' delivers it in a much more encouraging way.

> 'I respect your feedback, and we never have issues with
> our products.'

Here, the first truth is valued just as much as the second. The word 'and' encourages the listener to accept the praise, and it's then more than likely that they'll investigate the second truth or explore the behaviour you wish to change, without a feeling of failure.

'And' is like taking an alternative, more enjoyable route on a road trip: you still arrive at the same destination.

• • •

To practise empathy is to practise removing obstacles for people and breaking down barriers between you and those you serve. Turning your attention outwards towards others is about emptying yourself, getting out of your head and serving from your heart. When you let go of your ego and identity, you allow others to be seen and heard in a way that shows them you care. As legendary Zen Buddhist teacher Thich Nhat Hanh says in his book *How to Love*, 'Understanding is love's other name. If you don't understand, you can't love.'

Understanding the person you're serving, and their challenges or pain points, is the best gift you can give in service.

When you're more empathic, you're more successful in service.

Service Habit 10
SEE THEIR WORLD

Reflect now

- What gets in the way of you being empathic and 'seeing' people?

- How do you know when you're being empathic? What clues do you get from people?

- What's it like to be on the receiving end of your service?

Embed the habit

Literally or metaphorically, place an empty chair in your working environment to represent the customer at the centre of your thinking. Use the question 'What's it like to be you?' to look through the customer's lens.

If it's not possible to use the empty chair technique in meetings and team briefings, what else could you use to remind yourself and your team of what your customer might say if they were present? Get creative and set up a symbolic reminder to ensure that team members try to get inside the customer's head.

Service Habit 11
LISTEN TO UNDERSTAND

There's a hospital in the northern part of Australia that has trialled robots in its workforce. 'Pepper' is a robot that acts like a concierge, providing patients with information about the hospital. Pepper also followed nurses on their rounds, checking in with patients and asking questions to uncover anything they may need. While Pepper has no pulse, she won the hearts of many patients. I understand that the hospital surveyed the patients and discovered that a large proportion of the elderly patients preferred interacting with Pepper over interacting with the human nurses – they felt a greater connection with the robot! Statements from patients included:

- 'I was delighted with the one-on-one attention.'

- 'I was made to feel important.'

- 'When I had a question, Pepper responded in a way that made me feel heard and understood.'

During an interview with ABC News, one patient, Mr Rodney Whiting, even indicated that Pepper had some 'sass'. He joked, 'She is not backward about coming forward. I asked her a smoking question and I got the lecture about smoking.'

We're hearing more and more from futurists that the robots are coming. The truth is, they're already here. So, rather than viewing them as a threat, perhaps there are a few things we can learn from them. The intelligence that's built into machines these days to respond to questions and to offer solutions based on programmed scenarios is incomprehensible, yet the response to Pepper reminds us that we must not overlook another important attribute: their ability to give people unwavering attention. Those patients felt a connection to a machine with no heart, while the nurses with hearts didn't create the same connection.

People want your undivided attention, so give it to them.

According to John Dewey, an American philosopher, 'The deepest urge in human nature is the desire to be important.' When people feel understood, like the patients who interacted with Pepper the robot, they feel that they're important.

When it comes to listening effectively – meaning, listening to understand the other person rather than listening to contribute to the conversation – humans have a slight disadvantage to robots: we have minds. Our minds present a couple of barriers to effective listening, which means we humans have to work a little harder than a robot.

TWO BARRIERS

There is a variety of barriers to effective listening, such as noise, technology and interruptions. Before you blame external distractions or influences, though, consider this: there are two barriers that compromise your ability to give people your full attention in a way that makes them feel important, and both barriers come from your mind. They are:

1. your preconceived ideas

2. your need to contribute.

Understanding that these barriers exist is the first step to becoming an incredibly effective listener.

Giving people undivided attention is a matter of the mind first.

Your preconceived ideas

When you've been serving people for a while in your workplace, you'll naturally be influenced by previous experiences, so preconceived ideas are common in a work environment that is familiar and routine. They're subtle: if you're not watching for them, you may never realise just how automatic it is for you to make up your mind before an interaction has even commenced.

However, if you stereotype a person or make assumptions about their needs, you become less objective, less curious and therefore less likely to listen effectively. Think about it:

· When someone phones, do you start to formulate an opinion about the call before answering it?

· When a member of your team who typically acts like a know-it-all attends a meeting, do you decide the meeting will be a waste of time?

If you come to a situation with an agenda or a bias – even an expectation – you make assumptions and reach conclusions that can cost you an opportunity you may not have known existed.

Your need to contribute

A need to contribute often comes from a place of trying to be efficient, solution-oriented and, in some cases, simply wanting to add value to a situation for someone. However, it can be counterproductive to effective listening and ultimately to developing a relationship.

Most people are in one of two states during a conversation: they're either speaking or waiting to speak. 'Waiting to speak' is a bad, perhaps unconscious listening habit – it means you're thinking about what you want to say. You're unable to fully tune in and give focused attention to the person who is speaking. Your attention is divided between what they are saying and what you are going to say next.

Why do we do this? What's the motivator for wanting to contribute so quickly in a conversation? Why can't we be okay with letting people speak and waiting our turn?

The fifth habit in Dr Stephen Covey's *7 Habits of Highly Effective People* is 'Seek first to understand, then to be understood'. Covey explains that most people do not listen with the intent to understand; they listen with the intent to reply. When they do respond, often the response is one of the following:

- *Evaluating* – judging and agreeing or disagreeing
- *Probing* – asking questions from their own frame of reference
- *Advising* – giving advice and providing solutions to problems
- *Interpreting* – analysing what they hear based on their own experiences.

Looking at these four ways in which Covey describes our listening responses, you can see that having a clear intent to seek to understand your customers is not as easy as you thought!

We all have ideals and values that we believe to be correct, and it can be difficult to open up to others' contradictory views. Our ego loves to be in control – always thinking, figuring things out and validating its existence – and the more we buy into our ideas and beliefs (what the ego is telling us), the more we feel the need to share them. The consequence is that, when we're in conversation with colleagues and customers, sometimes our values and beliefs speak louder than theirs. It's like our mind is talking to us through a megaphone. So, we begin to mentally rehearse our response, and perhaps try to memorise key words, phrases or examples the other person is using. All the while, the person is still speaking – and if we're not careful, we can give off signals that our attention isn't fully on them.

How can you tell that someone's waiting for you to finish talking so that they can speak?

- They may lean in, indicating with their body language that they want to speak.
- They may pull a facial expression that shows you they have their response ready to go.
- They may bluntly jump in while you're mid-sentence and start talking.

They're telling you, loud and clear, that they've stopped giving you 100 per cent attention.

> *When you need to always be contributing, you close your mind.*

• • •

The two barriers of preconceived ideas and your need to contribute block your ability to listen effectively and serve from the heart; they keep your mind closed and opportunities minimal. Consider the following questions:

- How often do you have an agenda that you hope to achieve in a conversation with a teammate or customer?
- When that conversation doesn't go the way you hoped, do you let that become your focus, or are you still able to focus on the other person and give them your full attention while they speak?

- When you step in to serve people at work, are you trying to fix them, change them or even control them? Or are you sincerely and simply there to serve them, understand them and make them feel important?

If you are aware of your preconceived ideas and your need to contribute, and can let these unconscious tendencies go, you'll have deeper and longer-lasting relationships with people. You must ensure that they feel you're genuinely interested in understanding them and have the ability to get out of your own way, and being patient, willing, loving and self-aware is key.

Making people feel that they're important and have been understood is the essence of great service.

A NEW INTELLIGENCE

One of the core attributes required for strengthening any relationship is a truly open mind – wanting to understand people and learn how they think about things differently to you. Only when you are willing to openly listen and hear the other person's truth – rather than focusing on how you want the conversation to unfold or how you expect the sale to turn out – can you start to understand someone.

When you're serving people, there's sense in doing less than you may think is needed. Arrive at a conversation with curiosity and humility, intending nothing more than to simply listen and understand. There is always something new to learn in a conversation if you are able to 'get out of the way' and, in the moment, receive what this interaction is teaching you. You don't have all the answers, nor do you need to have all the answers. Carl Jung said: 'Everyone you meet knows something you don't know but need to know. Learn from them.'

Here are two simple ways of paying 100 per cent attention, maintaining curiosity and letting go of ego, so you get to the core of what it means to really serve:

1. Let the other person speak first and speak more than you do.
2. Practise silence.

You can start doing these two things immediately: with colleagues in meetings or corridor conversations, when you're working with people onsite or you're on the shop floor, with customers on the phone or in person, whether in brief, fast-paced interactions or in longer sales conversations. Watch: with these two practises, you will develop stronger listening skills, and this will provide a powerful advantage in any conversation.

Let the other person speak first and more than you

To serve without humility is to presume you have a right to evaluate, judge and control a conversation. Each of these is an act of dominance.

The first step towards humility is letting the other person speak first. By allowing others to speak first and more often, you're showing them that you believe their contribution is important. Humble listening may make you feel vulnerable at first, and it may appear weak – but it's not. When you have conversations with humility, you're checking your ego, your need to speak and your urge to contribute for the sake of it.

Serving others is a gift, if you choose to see it that way. No matter how predictable you may think people are, you will be challenged by the fundamental indeterminacy of human interaction. People change, and so do ideologies. Practise humility by allowing other people to do most of the talking, and you may be surprised.

Daniel H. Pink, author of *To Sell is Human*, reminds us to aim for a balanced speaking-to-listening ratio. While most people speak at only 125 to 150 words per minute, we can listen at up to 450 words per minute. That means you have time to listen.

Practise intentional silence

Most of us feel awkward sitting in silence. Can you recall the last time you allowed a pause to last longer than felt comfortable in a meeting, a conversation or on the phone? Do you always feel a need to fill in silent pauses?

I think there is silence and then there is intentional silence. When we are silent because we're simply empty of any idea, not sure what to say next or scared of opening our mouths, this can feel awkward. When our silence is intentionally giving someone space to think and express themselves, however, this can feel supportive, caring and kind.

There's sense in intentional silence. Not only is it courageous and caring to give someone space, sitting in silence is crucial to presence. In her book *Presence*, Amy Cuddy says, 'For some of us, it also means we need to overcome our fear of silence – of space'.

I encourage you to resist that urge to speak and just watch what happens when you allow more space and time for others. What do they say, reveal, express? What do you learn by simply doing nothing and being okay with silence? Certainly, people on the receiving end of intentional silence notice and appreciate the impact it has on them; see what you notice.

> There's an old adage, 'A leader speaks last'. I think, in service, we should speak least.

Service Habit 11

LISTEN TO UNDERSTAND

Reflect now

- When do you feel most understood and important to people?

- How can you come back to paying attention to others when your mind starts to prepare answers and get carried away with preconceived ideas?

- What's a great example of a time when you responded too quickly and missed the point?

Embed the habit

At the end of the day, check in on how well you tuned in during the day and how you made people feel:

- Who did you speak to?

- How many conversations did you have?

- How much silence was there in those conversations?

- Who spoke the most?

- How do you think people felt when they left their conversation with you – important or unimportant?

Service Habit 12
SQUINT WITH YOUR EARS

Some of the biggest challenges reported by teams in banks, stadiums, retail, airports, food and beverage and the mining and resources sector are communication challenges, such as listening and attention. Can you relate?

· You're often dealing with many people at once, trying to listen to more than one conversation at a time.

· Your work environment is loud and distracting. I've walked into offices where a television or radio is on as well, which adds another layer of noise to listen over.

· You serve many people all day. Without regular micro-breaks, food and plenty of water, it's hard to have the energy to keep paying attention and listening in the gaps.

· You feel a sense of urgency to serve people quickly, so you move at a pace that sometimes doesn't allow for effective listening. You're more focused on doing.

Think about something you really want to narrow in on. Focus on something you want to see clearly. In a busy service environment, it's very difficult to stay present and listen all day, which is why tuning in to what you hear beyond the words is just as important.

PEOPLE JUST WANT TO BE HEARD

I've heard countless stories from people I work with in the service industry about customers who want more than a product or service. They want to be heard. Here are some examples:

- The 70-year-old customer who visits his bank branch every Friday and tells all the staff about his time in a bank, when he, too, was a teller.

- The busy, multitasking mother having a bad day who calls her insurance provider to review policies, and ends up thanking the sales agent on the other end of the phone for listening to her worries and fears about the future.

- The excited football fan who attends every game of the season with his young son, interacting with a food and beverage attendant about some footy controversy – loving the banter as much as the game.

As much as service is about solutions and providing customers with answers, it's also about leaving people better than you found them – and that may sometimes mean just listening to them for the sake of listening.

It takes more than great products and services to create a positive experience for customers, too: you also need motivated, empowered frontline employees. One of the most effective and lowest-cost ways to build employees' commitment to superior service is – guess what? – to listen to them.

Leading companies have mechanisms to help them better listen to their employees on an ongoing basis. A 2016 McKinsey & Company article, 'The secret to delighting customers: putting employees first', reported that one Latin-American bank achieved a double-digit improvement in profitability per client by putting their employees first. Putting significant effort into listening to and thoroughly understanding their employees ensured that their employees' needs were met, which enabled them to deliver a higher quality of customer service, and this was a key factor in their results.

When employees feel heard, they will listen more deeply to their customers.

BEYOND WORDS

Except in email, the majority of our direct communication is probably nonverbal. We glean a great deal of information about each other without saying a word; even over the telephone, you can learn almost as much about a person from the tone and cadence of their voice as you can from anything they say. When I talk to my best friend, say, it doesn't matter what we chat about: if I hear laughter in her voice, I feel reassured that she's doing well.

With the working-from-home revolution and many professionals now serving customers and employees from a Zoom room or an online videoconference, it is sometimes tempting to turn the camera off and treat a video conversation like we would a phone call. There's a missed opportunity here. Speaking with cameras on gives people a greater chance of picking up nonverbal cues (even if they are sometimes a little pixelated). We want to give people every chance to communicate beyond words.

Face to face with a person, you get many more clues about what a person is communicating. You can detect enthusiasm or frustration very quickly in the expression around the eyes, the way they hold their mouth and their posture. When you're listening, remember that words convey only a fraction of the message, and pay attention to the nonverbal cues.

Equally, if you were to watch yourself converse, interact and serve people on camera with the video's sound muted, what story would you see being conveyed? What messages are you sending, without words, when you're listening?

Here are a few clues that indicate when people are not listening to you:

- They make no eye contact.
- They seem distracted – fidgeting, doodling in a notebook, looking at their watch, yawning.
- Their responses seem offbeat, and they have inappropriate facial expressions.

So, straight away, we can see that listening is not just about using our ears but also using our eyes.

When you're face to face with someone in a service environment, you listen with your ears – but you also look to see how they respond. This tells you quickly whether they're giving you their full attention or not. Although a level of interpretation error can be expected with nonverbal signals, how they make the person on the receiving end *feel* is also important.

In service, listening is the magical currency: it tells customers that you care. In service scenarios, the main aim of the game is to build rapport and show that you're interested in the other person.

Your nonverbal signals often speak louder than words.

LISTEN DEEPLY WITH YOUR EYES

Most of the time we listen with only one of our senses: our hearing. Your ears will only tell you so much, however, and if you rely solely on them, you'll miss most of what's being communicated to you.

The issue is that people will rarely tell you about their needs directly, and so it's up to you to listen beyond the words. There's a big difference between this and what we call 'hearing'. Hearing is effortless and involuntary, in many cases. If you have the gift of hearing – that is, you can perceive sounds through the vibration of your ears – then you probably hear things all day, and sometimes you hear things accidentally. Listening, by contrast, is intentional: as we discussed in the previous chapter, it's a conscious choice that you make to tune in and focus on what another person has to say. When you listen rather than simply hear your customers and internal stakeholders, it sets you apart.

We all know someone who's a great listener. They hang on your every word; they're present. It makes you feel pretty good, doesn't it? When you listen, you're present, which means you can listen for opportunities to build greater connection and trust and opportunities to sell a product, upsell or deliver an improved experience.

Listening with full receptivity involves letting go of your own internal dialogue and receiving what your customer or teammate is saying, remaining open and responsive to their comments and ideas. Research conducted by Judith E. Glaser, author of *Conversational Intelligence*, indicates that when we listen deeply, we activate mirror neurons. As we learned in Service Habit #10, these mirror neurons give us the ability to not just understand what another is thinking but to feel what they're feeling as well.

Therefore, deep listening leads you to deep empathy for those you serve.

USE YOUR SENSES

I think of listening effectively as being like squinting your eyes when you're focusing on something: you're really paying attention and narrowing in. I learned the phrase 'squint with your ears' from Perry M. Smith, a retired major general of the U.S.

Air Force. It's a term he used to teach his sergeants to listen – implying that you need to tune into all that you hear and see, rather than limiting your listening to what you hear.

In other words, you need to learn to listen with all of your senses. In some cases, you may draw upon the senses of smell or taste to give you greater clues about a situation; however, the following four senses are almost always relevant when it comes to deep listening:

1. *hearing* – what's being said, and what tone is being used?
2. *seeing* – what's the person doing with their body while speaking?
3. *instincts* – for example, do you sense that the person isn't communicating something important?
4. *heart* – what do you think the other person feels?

Listen in such a way that others love to speak to you.

PARAPHRASE

When you've accidentally stopped listening and tuned out, and you know you've missed important information, it's time to employ one of the most underutilised techniques in service – paraphrasing. This will not only slow you down and keep you focused, it will also clarify what you haven't heard.

You repeat back the person's words, trying to capture their main thought or message. This not only shows the person that they have been understood, it also adds an element of emotional atonement that can disarm any aggression or defensiveness on their part, and it helps to avoid misunderstandings.

In task situations, regardless of whether it's with internal team members or customers, always restate instructions and messages to be sure you understand them correctly.

BREATHE

The most effective tool you can draw upon, above all else, is your breath. Breathing exercises will help bring about a state of focused attention so that you can listen more carefully. They can also help you see things differently and make new choices based on this new vision.

To create a habit of breathing deeply and consciously, start linking three deep breaths to activities that you already do. This practice will help you become aware of when to use your breath during service interactions at work. So:

- Take three deep breaths before you get out of bed in the morning.
- Take three deep breaths when you turn the shower on.
- Take three deep breaths before every meal.
- Take three deep breaths before you start a meeting.
- Take three deep breaths before you get out of the car.
- Take three deep breaths before you go to sleep at night.
- Take three deep breaths before you serve a customer.

These three deep breaths will support your energy, and the habit will remind you to breathe deeply and listen consciously more frequently in general. It will help you in the gaps between speaking and listening. When you take this very small pause, you create a tiny space of silence: a better space to serve from. Just try it and see.

Service Habit 12
SQUINT WITH YOUR EARS

Reflect now

- Who do you know who's a good listener?
- Why do you consider them a good listener? What do they do?
- When do you find it most difficult to 'squint with your ears'?
- What helps you narrow in on a person and block out all other distractions so you can understand them?

Embed the habit

For at least one week, at the end of every conversation with your colleagues in which information is exchanged, conclude with a summary statement – paraphrase.

In conversations that result in agreements about future obligations or activities, paraphrasing will not only ensure accurate follow-through, but it will feel perfectly natural.
In conversations that don't involve agreements, if paraphrasing feels awkward, just explain that you're doing it as an exercise.

Service Habit 13
TEST YOUR ASSUMPTIONS

'Don't judge a book by its cover' is a well-known metaphor among various cultures and age groups for 'Don't assume'.

There's a famous scene in the movie *Pretty Woman* in which Julia Roberts' character, who is starting to make the identity transition from a working girl to a refined lady with expensive taste, is asked to leave an upmarket dress shop by the shop assistant. You may recall (and if you haven't seen the movie, it's worth a watch, for sure) that the next day, she drops back into the dress shop wearing a stunning white dress and white gloves, presenting herself like a lady with money. She tells the shop assistant what a big mistake she made and leaves her with her jaw open, watching the missed sales walk out the door. Assumptions can be dangerous and lead us into all sorts of hot water – especially when dealing with the general public!

FACT VERSUS FICTION

Assumptions start with incomplete information and an unwillingness to ask questions to complete the information. In the absence of data, we make up stories. It's not that we 'tell stories' like Pinocchio, in that we tell lies; rather, when we see something that looks like a familiar pattern – a familiar story – we make assumptions.

In a service environment, making assumptions can have small consequences, such as making people feel isolated or left out, and large consequences, such as limiting people's potential and development. These assumptions can include, for example:

- assumptions regarding age – like assuming that a senior employee's technology capability will not match that of younger workers
- assumptions regarding gender – such as assuming that women are better at making coffee
- assumptions about someone's education level – like assuming that it's difficult for a person to learn quickly, and therefore not including them in a training program.

When you assume, you fill in the blanks with your own interpretation of what you're seeing or experiencing: an interpretation drawn from past experiences that were similar. The problem with this kind of 'jumping the gun' or 'getting ahead of yourself' is that your solution to what you think the issue is could be completely irrelevant.

If an assumption involves another human being (whether customer or colleague), you are limiting your communication and your level of curiosity in that person. You're sending a signal that you're not that interested in them, and this will diminish what you learn and understand about the person.

Assumptions lead to major problems and regrets, and can impact relationships in an instant.

In general, when you make assumptions during a service interaction, you are preventing the need to communicate. When you're busy and rushed off your feet, you can subconsciously try to find shortcuts to get tasks done quickly. More assumptions lead to more complaints, though, which means more costs.

CURIOSITY IS THE KEY

In his bestselling book *Blink: The power of thinking without thinking*, Malcolm Gladwell explains that we all make assumptions, all the time. Sometimes we get them right, he says, and sometimes we get them wrong. Gladwell suggests that one of the reasons we continue to make too many assumptions is due to the pressure to make snap decisions.

As a starting point, to test your assumptions it's useful to ask, 'What evidence or facts do I have to lead me to this assumption?' This requires you to slow down your thinking and get deeply curious about the other person. According to a study published in scientific journal *Neuron* in 2014, the brain's chemistry changes when we become curious, helping us learn and retain information better. When you're curious, you're more likely to:

· stay in control of unexpected or unpleasant situations

· avoid communication problems with staff and customers

· reduce mistakes such as providing incorrect products or the wrong level of service.

Becoming curious is like training yourself to have a beginner's mind at work: practising seeing other people as if for the very first time, even if you know them very well. 'Beginner's mind' is part of a Zen theory that each moment is brand new. Thus, you should adopt a beginner's mindset in each experience, regardless of how many times you've repeated it in the past.

I interviewed a group of bank tellers on this topic, and they told me how well they know their customers, to the point that the minute a customer walks into the branch, the tellers have already decided what they need. Now, don't get me wrong – I'm all for advocating getting to know your customers well and thinking ahead. However, we never really know what's going on for another person, and just because we see a familiar face doesn't mean we should, without evidence, believe that we know what they need.

The point is, it's normal for employees to make assumptions about their customers, but the dangerous part is this: they often don't realise they're doing it.

TRANSFORM ASSUMPTIONS INTO QUESTIONS

To help minimise assumptions, you need to get good at transforming assumptions into questions.

Ask yourself a series of questions to reinforce that the story you are making up is just that – a story. Here are some of my favourites, which I have learned from people who are great at being curious:

- What do I need to learn and understand better about this situation?
- What do I know objectively?
- What additional information do I need?
- What questions might help me clarify?

Choose a question that is going to give you information that you don't currently have – information that will give you the best chance of making an informed decision.

> *When you notice you're making a casual assumption, you then have the opportunity to eliminate confusion.*

TEST YOUR ASSUMPTIONS

Reflect now

- When and in what situations do I make more assumptions than normal?
- How have assumptions got me into trouble in the past?
- When is it okay to assume?

Embed the habit

Spend a week watching out for when you make assumptions: make a note of every assumption you have made over an average work week. Ask yourself:

- What facts do I have to prove this thought is true?
- What facts do I have to prove this thought isn't true?
- What is a more realistic, middle-of-the-road way of seeing this?
- Is this really my own opinion, or did someone else teach it me and I didn't question it?
- Is this even really what I think or want to think in the future?
- What would life be like if the opposite of this assumption were true?

Service Habit 14
ASK BETTER QUESTIONS

How many times have you walked into a retail store and been greeted by a half-asleep shop assistant who says the classic, predictable and incredibly impersonal line, 'Hi, can I help you?' Or worse, they make a statement that isn't even really a question, such as, 'You're right to browse, aren't you?' It feels like they really don't care, even if they do.

Dale Carnegie advised, in his 1936 classic *How to Win Friends and Influence People*, 'Ask questions that other persons will enjoy answering.' More than 85 years later, most people still fail to heed this sage advice. In service, we're either asking questions to get someone to buy from us or trying to persuade them to buy into something – an idea, a product, a change of direction.

Most of all, it's your job in service to help customers figure out what they want in the first place. You have to think of yourself as a detective and go looking for clues that will help you help the customer.

Your default should be to think in questions rather than in answers.

THINK IN QUESTIONS

When you're in service to others and approach conversations thinking in answers, you're at risk of misunderstanding and overlooking people's needs and the solutions needed. The consequence may be that:

1. you make assumptions
2. the person you're serving doesn't feel like you're genuinely interested
3. you're likely to provide an inaccurate solution or outcome.

When you think in questions, however, you maintain a curiosity and an open-mindedness that allows the other person to do more of the talking. You have a greater chance of understanding their needs and giving them a relevant solution. If you think in questions, the benefits are:

- you get clarity about the other person's position, situation or problem

- you immediately build rapport simply by allowing them to talk first, which naturally makes them feel that you're genuinely interested in them and their needs

- you can provide solutions that are more accurate and impactful.

Sometimes we feel that, as service professionals, we have a responsibility to 'know everything', and we get anxious if we don't have all the answers. The truth is, however, that to be a great leader of people, a great customer service agent or a wonderful service team leader, curiosity is one of the strongest character traits we can have. A service provider is doing their work when they possess:

- the ability to recognise a problem

- a mental habit of looking for ways to improve a situation or experience
- a willingness to seek alternatives when an experience or situation is not helping the other person.

It's more valuable to ask the right questions than to produce the right answers, yet we've generally been taught how to answer, not how to ask. Questioning is a critical skill that allows you to excel in influencing, persuading and inspiring others to buy in.

CLOSED QUESTIONS

Like a bellows – a tool that feeds oxygen into a fire – you want to find ways to give oxygen to your conversations with people, and questions are the tool. But certain types of questions will feed a conversation more than others.

Closed questions can be useful to gather background information; for example: 'Have you been here before?' or, 'Do you have an account with us?' However, closed questions will typically only get you a yes or no answer:

- Do you want this?
- Is this what you want?
- If I do this, will you be happier?
- Can you finish this?
- Will you carry out the task the way we need it to be done?
- Is this how you expected the outcome to look?
- Do you know what to do?

Everywhere I travel, regardless of the industry, I see service interactions made up of dull, ineffective and counterproductive questions. No-one likes to feel interrogated or treated like a number or a task, but some types of questions can force responders into a yes-or-no corner. This syndrome of asking poor, somewhat lazy questions is also scattered through workplaces internally; busy, time-poor colleagues are directing and framing questions in the shortest possible way.

When you ask questions that generate yes or no answers – closed questions – they result in little information exchange. You don't get to the core of the issue or provide the right solution, because you have limited information. If you ask a poorly crafted question, there's a good chance you'll have to ask several follow-up questions to elicit the information you need in order to move forward with your colleague or customer. This could be avoided if the first question had been well thought through.

A *Harvard Business Review* article called 'The surprising power of questions' discussed research into survey design and how dangerous closed questions can be, in the sense of manipulating the answers you get. For example, when one group of parents was asked, 'What's the most important thing for children to prepare them in life?' and provided with a list of answers to choose from, 60 per cent of the group chose the option, 'To think for themselves'. However, only 5 per cent of the group came up with a similar answer when they were asked the same question in an open format.

You can shape an answer by the way you craft your questions; questions will either limit any possible spontaneity in answers or allow people to open up their minds and think for themselves.

If you ask a better question, you'll get a better answer.

OPEN-ENDED QUESTIONS

Open-ended questions allow the respondent to provide as much information as they like. They're particularly useful for uncovering information or learning something new. Open-ended questions allow you to:

- obtain information
- guide the conversation
- express your interest in the person
- clarify what the customer needs or wants
- explore a problem or a difficulty the person may be having
- encourage engagement in other products (not necessarily upselling).

Some of the most effective open-ended questions include:

- When did you shop with us last?
- Who are you buying for?
- What are you in the mood for?
- Where are you coming from today?
- How else can I help you today?
- What else might you need?

In the workplace, when you're relying on others to help you be your best professional self, or when your team is collectively solving problems for the customer or another department within the business, well-crafted questions can help you determine things like:

- how thorough a teammate's knowledge of a product or solution is before they begin
- how competently someone has completed a task
- the impact of their work and the outcomes for the customer.

In creating any employee or customer-service questionnaire or survey, as well as in face-to-face interactions, the more open-ended questions you ask, the closer you'll get to an authentic response. You can also:

· explore a teammate's potential next steps in relation to a problem they're trying to solve

· confirm a colleague understands the consequences of an unresolved situation

· allow your teammates to show you an alternative solution that you hadn't thought of before.

In service roles, you're always on the hunt for clues: open-ended questions are the way to fill in the blanks and tailor your solutions.

HOW TO CRAFT BETTER QUESTIONS

A helpful frame for asking better questions is to think about what question you could ask that people would enjoy answering. This service habit belongs to the pillar 'Understand others', remember, and the point of crafting a better question is not to show how intelligent you are, but rather to be more connected to and gain greater understanding of the person you are serving. Better questions expand a conversation rather than contracting it.

Here are four ways to start crafting better questions to help you achieve greater efficiency and better performance in your role:

1. Note and review your closed and open questions.
2. Correct and continue.
3. Work backwards.
4. Hold space.

Note your closed and open-ended questions

Draw a line vertically down the middle of a piece of paper, and write 'Closed' and 'Open' at the top of each column. Throughout the day, try to capture when you ask closed and open questions, and at the end of the day, go through your list and flip the questions to see how they might have worked differently. How could you have changed your closed questions to open-ended questions?

This builds your awareness of the two different categories, and also of how the intention of the question can change depending on whether it's asked in an open-ended or closed way – which means the answer you get could also change.

Correct and continue

If you find yourself asking a closed question that you know will get a yes/no answer, I encourage you to correct yourself and simply say out loud to the person in front of you, 'Sorry, let me ask you a better question…' People will see what you're trying to do – that you're respectfully trying to be better with your questions – and nine times out of ten they will go along with it.

Work backwards

When I prepare for a longer conversation, such as a client meeting, sales conversation or a session with a current customer, I try to put myself in their shoes when crafting my questions. This helps me get really clear about where to start the conversation. I think about how I want to leave them and what action I want to lead them to do. I ask myself:

·   What do I want them to know?
·   What do I want them to feel?
·   What do I want them to do?

Once I'm clear on these answers, I can then craft the questions to help me get there.

Hold space

'Holding space' is giving people the gift of silence, rather than speaking over them while they're thinking or deciding something. In Service Habit #11, 'Listen to understand', we saw the power of intentional silence – being comfortable in silence with a colleague or customer, not needing to fill the space with words but rather holding the space for what they need in that moment. This is service with grace. The space between our listening and speaking will often allow us to ask a better question when we next speak.

When you're holding space for inquiry, remember to:

· resist the urge to 'rescue' people

· avoid putting words into people's mouths

· pay attention to your body language, remembering that you're communicating even without words.

To have the greatest impact and persuasion in service, practise thinking in questions – better questions.

ASK BETTER QUESTIONS

Reflect now

- How well do you believe you frame questions?

- How would you assess the quality of your questions currently? Give yourself a rating between one and ten for your questions during interactions with colleagues and customers.

- Who asks great open-ended questions at work? What else do you notice about their question techniques?

Embed the habit

Start practising the four ways to craft better questions over the course of several weeks, and notice the practices you're strong at and those you need to keep strengthening.

In addition, make time to plan your questions every day. Here are my general rules of thumb:

- If I have an hour-long meeting, I set aside ten minutes to plan the questions I can ask to make that meeting most effective.

- If I'm serving many people in a day, I prepare a list of three to five well-thought-out questions that give me variety and depth, so that I'm not asking the same things of the same people all day.

- If I'm having a one-on-one conversation with a member of my team, I think about all the points I need to discuss with them and then convert each of these into a question, so I can understand more fully their knowledge and understanding of the topic.

Pillar 3
ACT
CONSCIOUSLY

THE FIRST TWO PILLARS have prepared you for what you're about to learn in this final pillar: to act consciously.

Acting consciously involves knowing that your behaviours throughout the ordinary moments in a day impact other people's lives. These last seven habits are intended to help you manage your behaviour when dealing with uncomfortable or unusual situations.

Get ready to:

· see how powerful language is, and how to leave lasting positive memories with people

· review your energy levels at work, and get sharp at maximising your time

· reflect on how well you're looking after yourself

· look at your level of flexibility and the adaptability of rules and procedures.

You might even find yourself smiling at the end of the last chapter and realising how simple this can all be when we're kind to ourselves.

Service Habit 15
PLAN YOUR CONVERSATIONS

One of the bad habits I developed when I was a General Manager in my corporate life was making a list of agenda items for a meeting. I say 'bad habit' lightly. Sure, it's good to be organised and know what you want to achieve from a meeting; however, I learned over the years from a great mentor that it's even better to turn that list of agenda items into a list of questions instead, as this will invite further conversation.

There's a saying, often attributed to Albert Einstein: 'If I had an hour to solve a problem and my life depended on the solution, I would spend the first 55 minutes determining the proper question to ask.'

Regardless of who we serve – our team or customers – we are always looking to solve problems. In order to act consciously when solving problems, it's helpful to think through a lens of questions.

TWO-WAY ENERGY

For rapport to be built in a conversation, both people need to feel there has been a two-way exchange of energy. Often, when a conversation feels one-sided, it's because someone has been doing all the giving and has left no room for the other to give. When you serve, a one-sided conversation may happen if:

- you're too wrapped up in the solution for the other person
- you're nervous (perhaps because it's your first day on the job or your first meeting with an important client) and want to impress the other person so badly that it gets in the way of basic chitchat and getting to know them
- you're really attached to achieving a specific outcome from the meeting or conversation.

People are often eager to impress others with their own thoughts, stories, opinions and ideas, and this can get in the way of building rapport.

> *Remember: the energy you invite from another person is just as important as the energy you bring to the conversation.*

It's not what you say but how you say it that allows the conversation to flow with real human connection. This applies when you're:

- in a sales meeting
- serving customers on the phone, via email or on a busy shop floor
- helping a colleague internally with a project
- hosting a team meeting
- conducting a one-to-one with a member of your team.

View these daily interactions as conversations, and allow the human you're conversing with to feel important. When you find a conversational vibe in your work, the person on the receiving end of your conversation feels that you're truly authentic – and that makes it feel like service, not selling.

Authentic, two-way conversations feel like service, not selling.

THREE KEY CONVERSATION STAGES

A conversation has a natural sequence: a start, a middle and an end. If you have a plan for your conversation with an intent for how you will start it, what the middle part of the conversation will be and how you'll know when the conversation has ended, then you can relax more. You are less concerned about what's coming next and more likely to allow yourself to listen fully and be present.

Now, plans don't always work out, but I encourage you to plan nevertheless, as a way of being prepared and ready for the important conversations in your workplace – knowing that they may not turn out that way and you have to be light with it. It's like planning for a holiday. It's great to have a plan, and it's even better to be willing to throw the plan out the window if it's no longer suitable or relevant. Either way, you feel more relaxed to go on the holiday because you've done your research and you have a plan.

As I mentioned, there are three stages to a conversation: the beginning, middle and end. For example:

- In a sales call or a simple service interaction, the beginning, middle and end would be *greeting, transaction and farewell.*
- In a team meeting, they would be *welcome, agenda and next steps.*
- In a coffee catch-up with a colleague, they would be *small talk, point of the meeting and thank you.*

When you witness the conversations of someone who's great at, say, sales interactions or conducting meetings, they appear effortless – as though it comes naturally to that person to balance the exchange of energy. They seem to allow the perfect amount of time in the interaction, getting what they need while still allowing the other person to be heard. They're masters of rapport – and a large component of forming rapport with others is being aware of energy and cadence in guiding conversations and reinforcing to others that they're important.

You want to arrive at a conversation bringing energy for all three stages. Let's look at these stages in more detail now.

1. Beginning

The beginning of a conversation is *the step before you speak*. Many people get this wrong: they think service starts when you open your mouth, but this is a huge misconception. Recall Service Habit #1, 'Choose to serve'? Service starts well before you see the customer or answer the phone to fix a problem. You want to start rewiring your thinking well before the other person is in your space, so that you're energetically prepared and open for them. Your energy introduces you before you speak: this is where the conversation begins, setting the tone and making the first impression.

I was trained in the McDonald's system, and it's a leading quick-service restaurant that has always believed in placing the customer at the centre of its operational procedures and pro-cesses. One of the standards we were taught in order to help us anticipate customers' needs and always have a 'happy to help' attitude was the 'Two-metre Rule'.

The Two-metre Rule is widely known in the hospitality industry and is a core principle for creating a special customer experience. When I was taught the rule, it meant that every time a customer was within a two-metre radius of your physical space, you needed to acknowledge their presence with a smile or a greeting.

I agree that this is a good rule to follow when greeting someone; however, what are you sensing before the greeting? Sometimes you can rush into a greeting – jumping into autopilot mode with the intention of providing care and service, but without taking a moment to read the person and match your greeting to their needs. If you do this, you can potentially become transactional and robotic. This critical first step is where you start to test your assumptions, ask lots of questions and listen more, so as to get off to the right start.

There are two magic, silent questions that you should ask yourself before you open your mouth. The first magic question is to help you read the person's energy; the second is to help you follow the cadence of the exchange. These two questions will keep you focused on the person with a curious mind, and will enable you to create an emotional connection with them immediately and start a two-way exchange of energy.

Magic, silent question #1

The first magic question is:

What am I sensing about this person?

Pay close attention to their body language, facial expressions, mood and gestures. If they're talking to someone else, what does the tone and quality of their voice sound like?

Start asking yourself this question as soon as you're within a few metres of the person. Try it when:

- you're walking towards the cafe table where your client is seated
- you arrive in a meeting room, as people take their seats and start to settle in
- you see a customer park in the car park and head towards the front door

- you see a team member arrive at work and go to their workstation.

Do not compromise on this first magic question. It will shift you into a place of presence immediately and dial up your attention towards others.

Ask yourself this question as though you were in a foreign country where they don't speak your language. If you don't understand the spoken word, you become extremely attentive to all the other ways that people communicate – their body language, hand gestures, facial expressions, tone of voice, mood and attitude. You look for clues.

In the same way, practising the first question involves looking for clues so that you can quickly decide how to approach the other person. In many ways, it's an unspoken gesture of respect. This question allows you to tune into the energy of the person. By focusing on what you sense about someone and acting on that sense, you show them that you're fully present with them in this moment. How great does it feel to be on the receiving end of service from someone who's tuned in and curious about you, interested in you? It makes you feel like they care, doesn't it?

Magic, silent question #2

The second magic question is:

When's the right time to ask a question?

'Timing is everything' is a proverb that's relevant to many aspects of business and relationships. You can pose inquiries in an optimal way simply by timing them right. However, you can only judge the right time to ask a question after you've silently answered the first magic question. Once you sense what the other person needs, you'll be able to determine when you should ask a question to get the best outcome in that interaction.

Let's look at an example of a bank teller dealing with three different customers:

- *Customer 1* seems to be up for a chat; they want to vent and just talk at you for a bit. So, delay your question: wait patiently until there's a natural break in their monologue to find out how you can best serve them today.

- *Customer 2* appears to be shy and lacking in confidence – they're looking to you to start the conversation. So, ease into your question. Provide comfort straight away by asking a question that puts them at ease: maybe something unrelated to banking, something more human, like, 'How's your day been today?'

- *Customer 3* seems distracted and confused, and they don't really know what they want. So, question them promptly. Be helpful by directly asking a question that helps them focus and get clarity on what their needs are.

This second magic question is all about the tempo and cadence of the conversation. You want to always try to tune into what vibe the other person is giving off and then plan your approach based on the clues you observe.

Cadence is just as important in conversations with colleagues. Keep up the two-way exchange so that people feel heard and that they've expressed what they need, and that time has been allowed for all views to be considered.

For example, consider a team leader who's conducting a staff briefing for a team in need of some motivation. The leader might start the briefing with a question. Opening strong with a well-thought-out question will get the team to do all the talking straight up and vent any issues they have on their mind. Allow that to run its course at the beginning of the briefing – people are more likely to listen after they've expressed their views.

2. Middle

The middle of the conversation is where the main purpose and intent of the conversation is dealt with. This is where you get clarity and achieve common ground. At this point, you may still not have established very much rapport, so you may need to dial up the empathy. In fact, if you or the other person has done all the talking thus far, the conversation may feel like a monologue; this is a great opportunity to break down the walls and relate in a way that shows them, 'I'm just like you!'

So, how do you encourage more conversation? Through great questions, of course. Here are the silent questions to ask at this middle stage that will ensure you are solving the right problem:

- *How are we similar? (Commonalities)* Let's look at a retail customer, for example. The customer comes into your store with her three-year-old daughter. You, too, have a three-year-old daughter, and you instantly establish some commonality by asking some questions about her daughter, a topic you can relate to.

- *What's it like to be you? (Empathy)* Consider a potential home buyer who is coming through for an inspection. The customer comes through the property and you, the real estate agent, try to understand what their motives and priorities are in buying a home by finding out more about them as a person. What's the home going to be used for? What's the customer's price range, and what's important to them?

- *And what else? (Questions)* Let's look at a banking customer who has applied for a personal loan. The customer has told you the bare minimum about why they need a personal loan and what their current financial situation is. Before you move on into the transaction, you ask one final open-ended question: What else do I need to know?

The last question 'And what else?' is my favourite to ask before moving to the last stage of a conversation. It ensures that context has been exhausted. I especially ask this question when meeting a new customer or a new team for the first time.

3. End

When wrapping up a conversation, it's important to check in and notice the other person's energy and responses. You want to part ways having left a great impression, even if the conversation didn't have the outcome you would have liked. Bring an energy of gratitude to the conversation at this stage and note the other gains you've achieved.

The silent questions to ask at the end stage are:

- What have you gained from this conversation? *(Intent)*
- What have I gained from this conversation? *(Gratitude)*
- What do I need to let go of or action as a result of this conversation? *(Reset)*

There's always something to gain from a conversation if you view it as a two-way exchange. It could be language that you've heard the employee or customer use repeatedly – that's new information you now have for next time you meet. It could be feedback about some of their problems and how they view them, and now you're better prepared for the next time the situation occurs. It could be a converted sale, or a conclusion to an internal problem that you didn't expect. There's much to be grateful for, and this energy can shift the conversation from 'I came here wanting to get something' to 'I came here and I'm grateful that I did'.

Remember, in service, regardless of what material things people leave with, they most certainly also leave with a felt energy from your exchange.

PLAN YOUR CONVERSATIONS

Reflect now

- How do you plan for conversations?
- What's the impact when you bring a clear intention and questions to a conversation versus when you do not?
- Who do you know who does questions well? Why?
- What do you need to be more prepared and planned with your own questions?
- What energy do you bring to conversations?
- What intention are you bringing to conversations?

Embed the habit

To embed this habit, you first need to decide to use silent questions from now on.

Practise noticing things about people before you speak, and pay attention to *when* you ask your first question. Was your timing appropriate? Did they have more to say and you interrupted them? Did you wait too long to ask a question?

Practise this:

- in team meetings
- in corridor conversations
- when having lunch with your colleagues.

Service Habit 16
PRAISE EFFECTIVELY

When I first started my management training at McDonald's, we were taught to go on 'travel paths' (an observation technique that involved walking around the restaurant) regularly throughout a day. The purpose of this was to look for things that needed attention.

I remember one day standing in front of the counter looking at the restaurant through the customers' eyes and making a list of all the things I could see that were wrong. My list included things like:

· dust on the shelves
· two employees without name badges
· incorrect promotional material on display.

Then, a long-time loyal customer – an elderly gentleman, Mr Andrews, who bought breakfast from us five days a week – called me over to his table. He'd seen what I was doing and asked me to confirm that I was listing things that needed correcting. He then pointed out, as a loyal friend of the restaurant, several good things he'd noticed that morning. Things like:

· The coffee is always hot and never runs out.

- The staff are extremely friendly, and nothing is too much effort.
- The restaurant is warm and welcoming.
- The newspapers are always on display.

I'll never forget that brief interaction – it felt more like a positive intervention.

When we point out the good to others, we're reinforcing what we want to see more of.

BUILD WHAT'S STRONG

University of Pennsylvania psychologist Martin E.P. Seligman, a well-known advocate of positive psychology, has described its core philosophy as a 'build what's strong' approach that can augment the 'fix what's wrong' approach of more traditional psychotherapy.

In workplaces, we do not always see what is already strong and working well. We're more likely to notice what others could do to be better than to notice what they're doing well. This is due to the brain's 'negativity bias': it innately has a greater sensitivity to unpleasant news than pleasant news. The bias is so fundamental that it can be detected at the earliest stage of the brain's development. From the dawn of human history, our survival has depended on our skill at dodging danger, so the brain developed systems that make it impossible for us not to notice danger – and thus, hopefully, to respond to it.

So, we have to make an effort to notice and recognise the good – or sometimes our customers, like Mr Andrews in my previous story, may point out the positives of a situation before we can see it. Once we are aware of the strengths in our teams and the positive impact that people are having on customers, we have the most influential tool to build a positive service culture: praise.

PRAISE TO RAISE PEOPLE AROUND YOU

A *Harvard Business Review* article called 'The benefits of peer-to-peer praise at work' discusses a low-cost airline named JetBlue. JetBlue created a peer-to-peer recognition program in which workers could commend others for everyday contributions, as well as for exemplary work or effort. The stories of success were shared throughout the company on an internal newsfeed, and the recipients recognised were awarded points that they could decide how to spend. For example, they could elect to redeem the points immediately for a dinner or save them up for a bigger reward, like a cruise.

The data revealed that for every 10 per cent increase in people reporting that they'd been recognised, JetBlue saw a 3 per cent increase in retention of employees and a 2 per cent increase in employee engagement.

Here in Australia, one of my clients in the banking industry has followed a similar process. It has used its workplace platform to share company successes and stories and keep a healthy internal feed of employee recognition submitted by other employees. It saw:

- employee engagement rise and relationships strengthen within departments
- a rise in five-star ratings and compliments from customers
- how praise and recognition reinforced to other, less high-performing team members what 'good' needs to look like in service
- how motivating praise can be, encouraging staff to do more of the praised behaviour.

There is no doubt that a culture that supports praise will lead to high-performing teams.

Teams who praise and recognise the good behaviours of members:

- grow together
- raise each other up, not needing hierarchy or leaders to lift them
- have a healthy respect for shared and individual performance and accountability.

Teams who are unable to praise and recognise each other:

- grow apart
- rely on hierarchy and recognition from leaders only
- allow poor performance to go unnoticed.

  When people are performing at their best and having a positive impact, recognition of this motivates others around them.

But are we praising effectively and frequently enough to get this rise in the engagement and performance levels of our teams?

EFFECTIVE PRAISE

Perhaps you can recall a time when someone in your working life gave you praise or recognition. Typically, when you remember being recognised, it's usually because of the delivery – how effectively the praise was given. Now, let's be clear: giving people any sort of positive reinforcement or praise – ineffective or effective – is better than nothing at all. However, if you're reading this book, you are looking for ways to improve your relationship with people, and once you see how easy and impactful effective praise is, you will want to do more of it as you go about your day.

Ineffective praise is vague, praises the task and is infrequent. Saying to people, 'Good job, mate' (vague) or 'Nice work on the register' (task-focused) and leaving praise until a six-month performance review (infrequent) are examples of ineffective praise.

Effective praise is specific, praises the behaviour and is frequent. Examples include saying, 'Well done today with the customer, Mrs Jones' (specific) or 'You took real ownership of the issue and committed to resolving it right to the end' (praising behaviour), and giving praise as often as you can or as often as you see good service (frequent).

I spy for great behaviours

Remember the game 'I spy'? The secret to making workplace recognition a habit is to look for great behaviours to praise, rather than just telling people they've done a good job – which is a shallow gesture of thanks.

You're more likely to motivate someone to change their behaviours if you talk about these behaviours. Task-oriented conversations tend to be focused on a goal or performance standard, but behaviour-oriented conversations are more relationship-based and focus on the person's motivation and wellbeing. From my experience, when you're on the receiving end of behaviour-oriented conversations, you're more likely to remember the point being mentioned and be motivated to change, as table 2 overleaf shows.

> *Effective praise is like a positive, lasting memory: it stays with people.*

Do you see how praising the task is less emotive and meaningful than praising the behaviour? Imagine if you were on the receiving end of any of these examples of praise; which one would have more of an impact on you?

Table 2: Praising the task versus praising the behaviour

Praising the task	Praising the behaviour
Thanks for filling out the form correctly.	Thanks for being a great team player.
Thanks for taking that phone call right on 5 pm today, when we close.	Thanks for showing commitment and care right to the end today.
Thanks for checking with the customer to see if the parcel arrived.	Thanks for taking ownership with your customers.

You don't need to be a leader to praise, either. Everyone benefits from genuine praise and thanks. Recognition from a fellow team member – being told out loud that you're recognised and appreciated – brings an increased level of pride and validation. From my direct experience, peer recognition should be an organic expression of gratitude, not forced or planned but shared because it's deserved. You just need to make it more of a habit.

The best service cultures are made up of individuals who both take responsibility for their own behaviours and also care about their co-workers' behaviours – all in the spirit of service.

Three steps to praising effectively

Here are three steps that sum up how to give effective praise:

1. *Look for more opportunities to praise.* Create an environment that visually reminds you that you're on the hunt for great behaviours. Many of my clients build in ceremonies and

rituals to prompt and trigger them to find moments to praise. Remember, we're wired to look for what needs fixing and what's wrong, so think about adding prompts or visual cues, such as posting the desired behaviours on the wall, or putting up customer success stories around the office or on a community intranet. Examples of great behaviours, when visible for all to see, will go a long way to helping teammates notice the great work and behaviours of others.

2. *Praise specifically good behaviour.* From Service Habit #6, 'Be the change', you will recall that when behaviours are explicit in a team, people know what 'good' looks like and have a better chance of high performance. You want to always call out the behaviours you're seeing that have been defined as what 'good' looks like. For example, if being a great team player is defined as a good behaviour in the workplace, then when you see it in action, you might praise by saying, 'Hey Mike, I want to praise you for being a great team player this week during the final step in the project.'

3. *Praise often.* Why wait for quarterly reviews or formal check-ins? When you see good behaviour, take a moment to call it out. Real-time praise is the quickest way to support people and show you appreciate and acknowledge them, not praise a month after the event when it's almost forgotten. Give praise in informal and formal settings – and remember, when you give praise effectively in a team environment, there's a good chance that others will witness it, which reinforces to everyone what 'good' looks like. I reckon if you're a leader of a team and you praise someone each day, then you're well on your way to being effective with your praise.

PRAISE EFFECTIVELY

Reflect now

- In a business, who's responsible for giving praise or appreciation to employees?

- What does it feel like when you get recognised or praised for doing a good job?

- What's one example of giving praise based on a task and one example of praise for a behaviour?

- How do the two types of praise feel different to each other? Why?

Embed the habit

- Call out good behaviours in others at least once a day.

- A golden rule for recognition is that the earlier the recognition happens after an event, the better. Don't leave it weeks to mention to a colleague when they have done something great.

- Check if your company has a peer-to-peer recognition program that's tied back to company values and behaviours. If it doesn't, suggest one.

Service Habit 17
TELL THE TRUTH

Picture this: I was on the hunt for a $25 bottle of pinot noir for a mid-week catch-up with my girlfriend – nothing fancy, but good enough for us to enjoy with the meal she had gone to the effort of cooking. I walked into a local independent bottle store and told the service attendant exactly what I was after, including my budget. He straight away took me to a bottle of wine that was $15, and said, 'This pinot noir is one of my favourites at the moment, and I'd recommend it over any of the more expensive ones.' Can you believe it?

I bought the wine, and it was just as good as he'd said, leaving me feeling I could trust his future recommendations. I returned to the store the following week to thank him for that recommendation and to buy some different wine that was more expensive.

In customer service, honesty is the golden rule. Customers respect honesty, and it's what keeps them coming back.

HONESTY IS THE BEST POLICY

Honesty is the best policy – the most powerful way to deepen relationships with the people you serve is to be impeccable with your word. This is especially the case if things don't go to plan and your business is having to tell customers bad news.

I recall a client of mine in the insurance business explaining that most of their customer-service interactions involve telling customers bad news, such as informing them of a delay in a claim or denial of a claim altogether, or that their settlement expectations were not being met. Although communicating this information is not at all fun in a customer-service setting, in the long run customers appreciate knowing the facts and will feel that they are in good hands being serviced by a team that will tell the truth, regardless of the news.

Research published in 2018 by the *Journal of Experimental Psychology* looked at the consequences of honesty in everyday life. The research defined honesty as 'speaking in accordance with one's own beliefs, thoughts and feelings.' Some people may believe that being honest is an uncomfortable experience for both parties; however, it appears that most people who took part in the experiment enjoyed the honest conversations more.

Being honest in conversation also benefits you. The way you conduct yourself in a job is extremely important to being a person of integrity, and this ultimately impacts your self-esteem. If you know you're someone who always keeps their promises, you can look in the mirror at night and feel good about the human being you are and the values you bring to each interaction.

Perhaps you've told a little fib or white lie in a moment of stress or awkwardness. Then, you have to remember the little white lie you told and keep track of which version of events you have told to which people. How exhausting! No job is important enough to lie. Be honest with your customers and be honest with yourself.

WORDS MATTER AND CARRY ENERGY

The biggest difference between us humans and the rest of the animal kingdom is that we have language. Words shape our beliefs and drive our behaviour, deriving their power from our emotional responses to them. When you're tempted to twist the truth a little, remember that words will shape your reality and the reality you communicate. Every word you speak has an energy behind it – whether you realise it or not.

The words that we use carry so much energy and power – not just for other people, but for ourselves, too. Service is an exchange of energy, and the words we speak are symbols that represent an energetic vibration; so, when we use low-level words, we have low-level experiences, and when we use high-level words, we have high-level experiences.

For example, in the workplace, you can easily offend and disrespect people, create doubt or distrust and damage relationships by choosing the wrong words, which carry the wrong energetic vibration. Here's a simple example: 'Have a nice day.' It's one of the most common phrases in customer-service interactions, yet how many people mean it when they say it? It's one of those autopilot responses that people throw in at the end of an interaction, sounding almost robotic or singsong. I question the genuineness of someone who says 'Have a nice day' if they say it with zero eye contact or no smile, or as they turn away to start their next task.

However, if I hear, 'Enjoy the rest of your day,' and it's said with eye contact and body language that are congruent with the words, and the energetic vibration of the words is uplifting and genuine, I feel that the person means what they say.

In simple terms, it's not just what you say; it's also how you say it. Nonverbal communication needs to match the words you speak to create trust and loyalty. Words that are delivered with mismatched body language, facial expressions or tones of voice can communicate the opposite meaning.

Words matter. You have the power to impact people greatly – positively and negatively – so switch on and pay attention to what you say.

SPEAK CONSCIOUSLY

How many times a day do you throw your words away? How many times in a week do you need to be direct with people, and maybe even blunt? How many times do you act so kindly that you avoid talking about something you really need to discuss? These are all examples of not being clean with your language. When you act consciously, you are clear on your intent and speak consciously. Telling the truth requires you to be consciously aware of the words that come out of your mouth, ensuring they are congruent with your true intention.

Throwaway words

I have a friend who's an Ishaya monk and has taken a vow to tell the truth. His aikido trainer always used to say to him, 'Say hi to your wife for me,' and he would answer, 'Will do.' Then one day, he thought about it and realised that wasn't the truth. He sometimes did and sometimes didn't pass on the trainer's hello to his wife. So, he decided to write himself a note to remind him to pass the greeting on. Later, he realised it was just as easy to text his wife at the time as to write the note. Finally, he decided, 'If my aikido trainer wants to say hi to my wife, he can just text her himself.' So now, whenever his trainer says, 'Say hi to your wife,' he simply says, 'Might do,' instead of 'Will do.'

What words do you throw away? Are they true?

Being direct and kind

My meditation teacher uses the term 'ruthless compassion'. What he's talking about is making sure that we are clear and direct when we need to be – and making sure we're not being so 'kind' that we avoid talking about what we need to or saying what the truth of a matter is. Brené Brown, in her book *Dare to Lead*, says something similar: she shows us that 'clear is kind'.

In work and in life, you will most likely be faced with criticisms and disagreements, particularly when you interact with people all day. How to handle yourself and maintain positive relationships is the art of a service professional.

Your job in service is to give people what will best serve them: sometimes this may appear a little ruthless, but it can still be delivered with compassion. 'Ruthless compassion' seems like a contradiction, yet it's one of the best approaches to dealing with mistakes, complaints and anything else 'negative'. 'Ruthless' suggests a fierceness – dealing with things in a warrior-like way. 'Compassion' is not just about being kind, but rather about doing the right thing for ourselves and for others.

Let's say you have to give a colleague some feedback or advice that they initially won't like hearing. Using ruthless compassion would mean you'd deliver the feedback in a way that isn't rude or mean, but at the same time doesn't enable them to get away with disrespectful behaviour. Eventually, they realise this was something they needed to hear and can see how it will serve them going forward.

In a customer scenario, I always like to think of ruthless compassion as taking a position of strength. Sometimes, you need to present the facts and help the customer see that they may be being unreasonable. However, Dale Carnegie, author of *How to Win Friends and Influence People*, suggests that a principle in the business of relationships is to 'let the other person save face'. His point is that even if you're right and the other person is definitely wrong, you only destroy ego by causing someone to lose face. You're better off showing them that you understand their point of view (empathy), and then calmly and compassionately presenting them with the facts.

You can maintain a relationship with someone without offending them or arousing resentment.

PROMISES AND PLAIN LANGUAGE

When it's all said and done, in any business, you're in the game of keeping promises.

Patagonia is an outdoor clothing brand that is held up as a great example of delivering on an exceptional brand promise. It promises its customers that it is committed to creating high-quality, long-lasting products, and offers a repair and reuse program for free. It even goes so far as to discourage customers from purchasing too many of its products. Patagonia's example shows that it's not enough to have your brand promise highlighted on your website and in store: each individual employee has a role to play in keeping that promise. This reminds me of the service attendant in the bottle shop who directed me to the less expensive pinot noir; it was that interaction with him telling the truth that made me a customer for life.

In service, you're under scrutiny, and honouring your promises (no matter how small) can earn you an enviable reputation for being reliable and trustworthy. So, when you tell your customers that you'll call them back later that day, do you? When you tell your colleagues you'll take care of the overflow of work for the week, do you? When you tell your manager you'll have a report to them by the morning, does it land in their inbox as promised?

Sometimes, you might not stick to your word. Maybe you forgot, you got sidetracked or distracted, you were stuck for time – or maybe you didn't realise you'd promised something in the first place. Regardless, if you become known as someone who promises the world but doesn't deliver, you'll lose face and trust and, over time, people will stop relying on you.

Don't be a promise-breaker. The easiest way to deepen relationships is to do what you said you would.

Say what you mean, and mean what you say. One common issue that confuses staff and customers is when acronyms and jargon are overused. People use acronyms and clever language with customers to appear knowledgeable, but they may as well be speaking a foreign language at times, and it can feel like they are showing off or perhaps even have something to hide.

When I worked with a particular bank to create an improved service culture, one of the issues raised was that staff were speaking a language customers didn't understand – using internal acronyms, jargon and references that were confusing and misleading. So, they decided that under their value of 'Authentic and Transparency', one of their behaviours for the future needed to be 'We use plain language'. This empowered staff to say what they mean in their own words, and not to feel they need to use the old companyspeak or try to sound clever.

Use language that describes reality rather than masking reality.

When you speak in code or riddles, you confuse people and put up barriers; and, in some cases, this will create a disconnection between employee and customer and cause people to distrust you. It also creates more work: you're forced to explain what you're actually saying, or deal with the resulting misunderstandings and errors. Just use plain language.

TELL THE TRUTH

Reflect now

- When have you been emotional and said something you didn't mean?

- What would happen if you slowed down a little and spoke more consciously? Would you choose different words? How much jargon are you bringing into conversations?

- If someone were to observe your communication with customers, would your body language and tone match the message you are intending to convey?

- How well are you sticking to your word and delivering on your promises to customers and colleagues?

Embed the habit

For the next 24 hours, pay very close attention to the promises you make.

Service Habit 18
LOOK AFTER YOUR SHAKTI

A client once said to me, 'I get to work at 7 am, I eat my vegemite sandwich at my desk and leave the office at 7 pm.' Sadly, I know she's not alone. In fact, in 2017, TSheets by QuickBooks commissioned Pollfish to survey 500 Australian workers about their lunch or meal break and found that almost a quarter of Australian workers power through the day without a lunchbreak. When asked why, 75 per cent of those respondents reported feeling that they couldn't enjoy a break because there was too much work to do and too few staff to do it.

Do you relate to this?

WELLBEING AT WORK

Employees who feel well are more likely to delight a customer. The focus on people's wellbeing in the workplace since COVID-19 emerged has increased significantly. Employee wellbeing has taken on a different meaning in the workplace, and most leaders are playing a more active role in caring for their teams.

Back in the '90s, employee wellbeing was defined as putting bowls of fruit in the staff lunch areas and ensuring office spaces had indoor plants. Eventually, workplaces evolved to include

R U OK? days and internally promoted Employee Assistance Programs (EAPs). Now, it appears that not only is employee wellbeing a stream of work with a plan and a budget, but there is also a new level of accountability and responsibility in providing greater employee wellbeing benefits and programs.

When a company creates a culture that takes care of its people, it essentially creates a culture that enables people to take care of their customers. For example:

- Employees who are present and mindful create greater connections with customers.

- Employees who can self-regulate (manage their emotions) manage difficult customers with ease.

- Employees who fill up their own cup first apply discretionary effort when needed.

- Employees who manage their energy levels serve the last customer like the first.

Wellbeing is the experience of health, happiness and prosperity. It includes good mental health, high life satisfaction, a sense of meaning and purpose, and the ability to manage stress. More generally, wellbeing is just feeling well.

Your employer plays a large part in your overall happiness and performance at work, and you have a responsibility to manage your energy as well.

Whatever you want to do better at work, it's about managing energy better.

SERVICE IS ENERGY (SHAKTI)

'Shakti' is a Sanskrit word that can be loosely translated as 'life energy'. Service is an exchange of energy, as we've discussed earlier, and the first energy you need to pay attention to is your own.

Many of us take a break as a reaction to a basic need like food or water; very few proactively stop work in order to manage our working time and energy. If you want to be able to serve your last customer of the day like the first customer of the day, though, you need to be good at energy management.

The human body is like a battery. If you were switched on all day, every day, with no recharge, then eventually your battery would drain and you'd come to a stop. In addition, your power supplies (your energy levels) would dip and rise throughout the day. Sometimes you have lots of motivation and energy, and other times you don't. Every once in a while, we can push through to meet a deadline, and this is a sign of dedication and commitment, but it's not sustainable over the long term.

It's important to pay attention to your personal energy patterns. For example, some of us rise early and feel energised throughout the day but wear out by evening, while others detest mornings and don't peak until late afternoon. This is called your 'chronotype', and it manifests in your circadian rhythm and sleep patterns. Once you know your rhythms, sleep patterns and chronotype, you know at what times of the day you have optimal energy levels and what times you don't.

If we understand our internal rhythms, we can learn to use them to our advantage.

Daniel H. Pink explains in his book *When: The scientific secrets of perfect timing* that most people describe themselves as either morning people ('larks') or evening people ('owls'). However, it turns out that the majority of us are somewhere in between: we're 'third birds'. Regardless, problems arise when we ignore our rhythms and try to maintain constant activity throughout the day, instead of heeding our need for regular breaks.

ENERGY MANAGEMENT OVER TIME MANAGEMENT

High performers in service pay attention to their daily energy rhythms in order to optimise their relationships – they know that people come before tasks and so try to maximise their peak performance where possible. Take a moment and consider the way you manage your energy state on a typical day.

Donna McGeorge, author of *The First 2 Hours*, suggests that we should do our most important work when our body and brain are most awake, alert and ready for action. Further, she suggests that tasks that have both a high intensity and a high impact on our results constitute our most important work of the day. From my experience, I'd suggest that serving people is always high intensity and high impact.

If you're a service professional who's based in an office, it's straightforward to be conscious about the time of day when you do your 'important work'. You can schedule tasks that require attention and focus (such as sales conversations and performance discussions) at your peak-energy times and leave the more repetitive, low-intensity tasks (like emails and routine meetings) for your periods of lower energy.

I find that the Pomodoro Technique, developed in the late 1980s by Francesco Cirillo, is a great way to work more productively when I'm in an office environment and have some level of influence over my schedule. It involves working for 25 uninterrupted minutes, then taking a five-minute break. You repeat this cycle four times, before taking a 15- to 30-minute break. It's a very effective way to manage your energy throughout the day.

What do you do if you serve customers all day long, though – on a shop floor, for example – and have no say over the timing of tasks? How do you stay awake, alert and ready to do your most important work: serving?

In a more fluid work environment where customers demand your attention all day long, all the time, discipline and scheduling tips in the world won't help – they don't suit the nature of your role or the demands of your customer. Instead of becoming an expert in time management, you need to find a way to become an expert in energy management.

STATE, NOT SCRIPT

Remember, service is an exchange of energy. As a service professional, you give your energy to others and others give their energy to you, so you need to protect and maintain your energy throughout the day. However:

- Customers want to be served by you when it's convenient for them, not when it's the best time for you based on your internal rhythm.
- Your boss and colleagues want to meet when there's a gap in the diary; they don't choose the time for a team meeting or a debrief based on your internal rhythm.

This means that you need to take responsibility for mastering your energy levels at work to ensure that every person you encounter is getting a fully charged version of you, regardless of the time of day. When you sacrifice your opportunities to recharge, you compromise the quality of service you give. Over the rest of this chapter, we'll look at ways to manage your energy to provide consistent, high-quality service.

The energy you bring to service is like the energy you'd bring if you were speaking on stage or speaking up in a meeting – you want your customers to connect with you, to believe in you. Think about times when you've gone to hear a professional speaker or listened to someone addressing the group in a team meeting; as part of the audience, you feel the speaker's energy from the stage or the front of the room, right? If they deliver words without feeling – inspiring words but with draining energy – then the audience doesn't connect with them and ultimately may not believe in them.

Matt Church is one of Australia's top conference speakers and has been named one of the top ten motivational speakers in the world by eSpeakers, the peak global event industry body. He talks about managing your *state, not script.* This means checking in with what you're transferring energetically (your state) from the stage (or the shop floor). The words you say (your script) are secondary to this.

Manage your state first when interacting with others. If you've prepared your notes and your key messages, you know what you want to convey. Your script is done, it's within you, and from there, it really depends on the energy state you're in and how convincingly you deliver the message. The energy state you transfer to people is what will impact them most and stay with them when you leave the room.

Whenever I prepare for a conference or a smaller meeting forum, I ask myself the same three questions I mentioned in the chapter on Service Habit #14:

1. What do I want them to know?
2. What do I want them to feel?
3. What do I want them to do?

Managing your state is about answering the second question, 'What do I want them to feel?' To manage your state, keep coming back to how you want to make people feel while they listen to you speak: excited, inspired, reflective, disrupted? It's a helpful frame to use when thinking about making your energy match the needs of the audience in the room, or the customer you're with, and managing the energy you wish to convey.

TAKE A BREAK

When you ignore your cycles of high and low energy, you make things worse for yourself, because if your energy is low but you're pushing yourself, that energy will just get lower, faster. If you're being reckless with your energy, then you're choosing to believe statements like these:

· 'If I keep doing more, I'll achieve more.'

· 'I can't afford to take a break today: I must push on.'

· 'I'm feeling tired and hungry, but there's no-one else here, so I'll keep going.'

By contrast, when you pay attention to your cycles and allow time for both recovery and hard work, the low-energy periods end sooner and your high-energy periods become really high energy; you become more productive. You choose to believe:

· 'If I slow down, I'll achieve more at a better quality.'

· 'I must find time to take a break today if I want to get the important work done.'

· 'I'm on my own today, so I need to eat a good breakfast and take lots of micro-breaks throughout the day.'

Whatever you want to do better at work, it's about managing energy better.

Regardless of the nature or location of your work, when you have the privilege of serving humans all day – customers or colleagues – you need to pay attention to how you're feeling. What are the indicators that it's time to take a break? Do you:

· feel irritable, impatient or unsatisfied?

· experience cravings or start checking texts, social media and email?

- have difficulty starting or finishing projects?
- notice that you're forgetful, making careless mistakes or feeling impulsive?

In *The First 2 Hours*, Donna McGeorge refers to three key factors that influence how you work and how well you work, based on your energy throughout a day:

1. *fuel* – as what you feed your body has a direct impact on your cognitive performance

2. *movement* – as exercising boosts your productivity and happiness

3. *rest* – as getting enough sleep allows you to stay motivated and make good decisions.

I agree that these three factors are a great place to start thinking proactively about how you can manage fatigue and energy at work, whatever type of role you have. In service roles in particular, however, taking a healthy approach to these three factors is crucial: it's the bare minimum for maintaining quality relationships. You need to serve yourself first.

So, the non-negotiables checklist for service professionals is as follows:

- Drink plenty of water throughout a day (at least two litres).
- Eat food that your brain loves, such as protein and vegetables.
- Minimise stimulants such as caffeine and sugar.
- See natural light or nature during the day, even if only for five minutes.
- Take breaks in which you get moving and have a change of scenery, rather than sitting at your desk or in your car.

- Schedule space in between meetings or serving people and set aside some downtime alone.
- Spend minimal time stationary – that is, don't sit at a desk for hours at a time.

When you serve yourself first, you have greater emotional self-control, which means you can create a gap between your emotions and responses, and respond in ways that are far more considered and of better quality.

Taking moments throughout the day to tune into how you feel is a productive habit. Maybe it's time for a short break now?

Ask yourself, what are you feeling right now as you're reading?

IT'S ALL ABOUT RECOVERY

I discovered a great episode of *The Tim Ferriss Show* podcast where Tim is talking to LeBron James and his trainer, Mike Mancias. James is giving Michael Jordon a shake for the title of greatest male basketball player in history. He's the world's first billion-dollar athlete, and he spends more than a million dollars a year looking after his body.

In the interview, James and Mancias kept coming back to the value of consistency and recovery. Consistent training rather than hard training, and a huge focus on recovery – including sleep, nutrition and hydration. It makes sense that LeBron James takes that kind of care of his body and his mojo. And I reckon it makes sense that you do too.

You probably don't have a spare million dollars a year to spend on your own hyperbaric chamber and a personal nutritionist to take with you everywhere. However, if you consider your work to be as important (or more) as playing basketball, and if your customers deserve it, it might be worth paying a little more attention to your recovery – to your sleep, nutrition, hydration and, of course, to your mojo.

There are ways of building recovery into your days that are effective and sustaining; from years of working with and surrounding myself with high performers in service, I've learned a few great techniques. Here are my two favourites; they've proven time and time again to manage my Shakti well if I commit to them.

1. Do emotional audits during the day

I love what I do and I stay extremely present with my clients: I can easily get carried away with work for hours on end. If I'm not disciplined in taking breaks every 90 minutes, I can burn out easily.

So, I set a timer on my phone for 90 minutes when I'm doing prolonged work, and when the timer goes off, that's my cue to take a micro-break. Before I take the break, however, I do what I call an 'emotional audit'. I ask myself the following questions, pausing for five seconds after each question to really tune in and listen to what the real answer is:

- What am I thinking?
- What am I feeling?
- What do I want now?
- What do I need to do differently now?

Then, I go and do what I need to do to shift my energy. This is a way of making sure I am acting consciously with myself. Checking in and asking myself these few questions allows me to get really present and be kind to myself before I move on to the next task.

2. Master your micro-breaks

A micro-break, for me, is a break of somewhere between five and fifteen minutes. During a micro-break, I might:

- stand up and go for a walk, preferably outside to get some fresh air
- take a seat on my meditation cushion and do some slow, mindful breathing – clearing my head and sitting in silence or with quiet music in my headphones
- make a pot of tea or filter coffee. I intentionally use pots and filters for hot drinks because they take time. I like to watch the coffee drip through the filter or the tea infuse in the teapot: it slows me down, makes me stop
- stand up and deliver a random act of kindness to a colleague or customer, just because.

Taking time for yourself isn't selfish or lazy; it ensures you're awake, alert and attentive for the important work – that which involves people. Learn to listen to your internal rhythm, honour what your body and mind is telling you and take the appropriate action to recharge.

Serve from a full cup, not an empty one.

LOOK AFTER YOUR SHAKTI

Reflect now

- What do you do when you go on a break? How do you recharge?
- What activities recharge you at work?
- What are some self-care practices that are effective for you when you're at work?
- How do you trigger your conscious mind to change your state?

Embed the habit

Create a menu of all the micro-break activities that would work for you: write them down and stick the list up somewhere visible in your main work area. This will act as a visual cue to get you thinking more about the quality of your micro-breaks and provide a heap of variety so you don't get bored.

Serve yourself first: others will reap the benefits!

Service Habit 19
MINIMISE MULTITASKING

Since the world has gone digital, online meetings, online learning platforms and online team gatherings have created a workplace environment that makes it easier than ever to multitask and be interrupted.

Smile and talk to me with your camera on and keep one eye on your inbox on the other screen.

Smile and talk to me with your camera on and place yourself on mute while you listen to a voicemail.

Smile and talk to me with your camera on and check your mobile phone, out of the camera frame.

Some of these behaviours we would just not do if we were in a room with others. We'd think twice and perhaps find a way to not be distracted if another human was in front of us, not on camera.

Think about all the distractions that can occur during your working day. These can be real traps for service professionals: they may be part of the reason many of us try to multitask. However, when it comes to human-to-human interactions, you must maintain focus and pay attention despite the distractions and interruptions. The question is, how?

MYTHICAL MULTITASKING

When you're with colleagues or customers, multitasking is not respectful or productive. People who multitask are busy; people who don't multitask are productive.

Confucius said, 'The man who chases two rabbits catches neither.' Experiments have been conducted in multitasking since the 1960s, and researchers refer to the 'processing bottleneck' which prevents the brain from working on key aspects of two tasks at the same time. In his book *CrazyBusy*, psychiatrist Edward M. Hallowell described multitasking as a 'mythical activity in which people believe they can perform two or more tasks simultaneously as effectively as one.'

Multitasking involves task-switching – consciously and completely shifting attention from one task to the next and focusing on the task at hand. Dealing with two or more tasks at a time is the main characteristic of multitasking, but when you try to do two tasks at once, you actually switch between those two tasks rather than doing them simultaneously. This switching back and forth leads to a slower completion time and more errors, meaning you're less effective. According to an article written by Paul Atchley for the *Harvard Business Review* and called 'You can't multitask, so stop trying', it takes an average of fifteen minutes to reorient yourself to a primary task after a distraction, and efficiency can drop by as much as 40 per cent.

People deserve your undivided attention when you serve them. If you don't provide it, you give the impression of not listening to them or understanding their needs, and so the relationship begins to fray. It's disrespectful to:

· speak on the phone while typing an email
· check emails while on a Zoom meeting

- speak with someone while texting someone else on your phone
- talk to a co-worker while serving a customer.

The human brain can only process one conscious thought at a time. So, if you choose to multitask when you're serving a human, you're choosing to serve them unconsciously.

Multitasking is a bad habit that damages relationships.

BUT IT'S MY JOB!

It's no secret that in many service roles, multitasking is described in the job description as an essential requirement. If I read this in a job advertisement or job description, I see it as code for 'highly stressful role'. More than likely, you'll be dealing with multiple communication channels (email, phone and databases, for example), and will be constantly switching between these channels and juggling competing priorities. This sort of approach is a recipe for errors, low productivity and exhaustion.

So, how do you get your job done without multitasking, even if it's part of your job description?

It's about learning to focus.

Paying focused attention means concentrating on your target and filtering everything else out. For example, you might be serving a customer, having a long conversation with a colleague or writing a report on your laptop. Attention is a limited resource: you can strengthen your focus by learning to filter out other stimuli and minimise distractions. So, set boundaries and make it clear where your focus lies. This isn't about being inflexible but about calling out the priority that you're committed to at a particular time and limiting distractions from it as much as possible.

I had a great leader once who taught me a very simple technique for being fully present with people, which I now try to practise when I'm with my team. If a colleague comes over to my workspace and interrupts me with something urgent, I'll acknowledge them and indicate I'll be with them in a moment. I finish the sentence I was writing or capture the thought on paper before putting my pen down or pulling away from the keyboard. Then, I turn my entire body to face the person, look into their eyes and say 'Hi!' I'm signalling that I'm fully with them, giving them my undivided attention. They have to wait a few seconds for me to do this, but they respect the intention.

Depending on the role you have at work and the tasks you do in a day, your boundaries may look different. Here are some tactics you may find helpful for staying focused if you're working in an office environment:

- Close your office door – and educate people that when the door is closed, it's because you need uninterrupted time.

- Schedule email time – educate your team that you check emails twice a day, once in the morning and once in the afternoon, so they don't expect you to respond every minute of the day.

- Turn off your notifications, and set your computer up so that the first screen you see in the morning is your calendar, not your email inbox.

- Don't answer the phone – turn on flight mode when you're serving someone or working on an important project or task.

- Put your headphones on – I only listen to instrumental music, so there are no lyrics for me to be distracted by.

Where you put your attention is where you live. So, where are you placing your attention when serving others?

Tactics for minimising multitasking

Here are some tactics you may find helpful if you're working on a shop floor or in an operational environment:

- Answer the phone or send it to voicemail – if you're serving a customer face to face and your phone rings, step away from the person you're with and either take the call or send it to voicemail. Don't try to do both at the same time.

- Make a list of things to be done that don't involve serving customers – I find the more stuff I get out of my head and onto a to-do list, the more focused and present I am when I'm with people. I know the list is there when I need to refer to it, so I can fully concentrate on the person in front of me, rather than trying to remember things in my head.

- Stop doing whatever task you're doing when a customer walks into your space. You want to give people your undivided attention, and a very conscious way of doing this is to stop your task when they're nearby.

- When you are on a break – break! It's professional to be away from customers and off the shop floor when on your break. It's also ideal to not be in uniform, so you can fully switch off and recharge the batteries for when you return.

Picture a busy host in a restaurant:

1. She's talking to a customer seated in the dining room.
2. The restaurant phone (which is in her back pocket) rings, and at the same time a new customer arrives at the front desk.
3. The host excuses herself from the first conversation, nods and smiles at the new customer to acknowledge them, then stops walking towards the new customer and answers the phone.

4. She warmly greets the person on the phone and asks if they would mind holding for a moment.

5. She delegates the phone call to another colleague who has just arrived on shift.

6. She walks directly to the new customer at the front desk, gives him her full attention and greets him warmly.

At each step of this sequence, the host has focused her attention on what she is doing at that moment. If you were to watch this for real, you'd get the sense that the hostess is a productive worker; she wouldn't give off a frantic, busy energy. She has nodded and smiled at the customer at the front desk, so he knows she'll be with him shortly and feels seen and acknowledged. By pausing in her walk towards the new customer and taking the phone call, she indicates that she's focused on the call.

The alternative is that the host answers the phone while she's walking towards the customer at the front desk, and while she's on the phone, grabs menus and gestures to the customer to follow her to a table. If I were the customer at the front desk in this situation, I'd feel that the host was dividing her attention between me and a phone call, and I wouldn't feel confident or positive about the experience. What about you?

TOO BUSY TO SERVE?

Of course you're busy. That's life, right? Especially a life of service. The word 'busy' is thrown around loosely, but regardless of the unrelenting demands of your work and unforeseen demands of your life, you can choose to be busy or not. There is a healthier way of thinking about life, and it starts with reframing the word 'busy'.

I very rarely say or think this word, as it has a frantic, chaotic, panicky and almost apologetic vibe. I don't want my customers or team feeling like that! When I approach a full day, knowing there are many meetings in it, many customers to serve and much work to do, I simply tell myself, 'It will all get done'. This helps me deliver my messages with ease and intention, and without passing on a 'busy' energy vibe to others.

We're all busy – don't pass even more busyness on to others.

This service habit is an extension of looking after your Shakti (Service Habit #18). It's a great way of conserving energy: think about how you feel after you have been productive versus after being busy.

Remember, if you are choosing to multitask when you're serving a human, you are choosing to serve them unconsciously – which is the antithesis of acting consciously.

Rise above being busy and stop multitasking.

Service Habit 19
MINIMISE MULTITASKING

Reflect now

- When are you most likely to multitask?
- How does the quality of your work change when you split your attention?
- Why do you multitask? What choices are you making?
- What tactics might you try to minimise multitasking?

Embed the habit

Here's a focusing technique that is particularly good to do at the end of a day when you've had a lot going on:

1. Dim the lights and place an object in front of you to focus on – perhaps a lit candle or a plant.
2. Stare at the point of focus for 10 to 15 minutes.

Do this a few times throughout the week, then start to use this focused attention in your workplace – applying the same skill and discipline to people at work.

In your work environment, try the following:

1. When you're with people in meetings (online or face to face), turn off notifications on your phone. Phones are designed by lots of clever people to steal our attention. We have to fight not to lose that battle.
2. Close your office door to make the most of uninterrupted time.
3. Never say you are busy ever again. Stop using that word as a badge of honour.

Service Habit 20
BEND BLUE RULES

My friend Pete and his two daughters Scarlett and Ami made it home by the skin of their teeth. They flew out of Argentina on a Wednesday (Buenos Aires to Rio de Janeiro to Dubai to Melbourne – 40 hours door-to-door) and by the Thursday, Argentina had shut down all commercial flights in and out of the country due to the global pandemic.

After 40 hours of travelling, during which he hadn't really slept, Pete got off the plane with five pieces of cabin luggage. Ami had lost it, so he was carrying her and four of the bags while Scarlett pushed the fifth bag.

They went to the luggage carousel and Pete collected their six pieces of checked luggage... but when he picked up the sixth, he looked at the tag and realised it was someone else's. He put it back on the carousel and watched it go around three more times – and then realised that David (the name tag on that bag) must have picked up his bag by mistake and left. So, Pete spent another 30 minutes queuing up and dealing with baggage services while managing two deliriously tired girls, before finally getting out.

Pete's wife, Trish, had arranged to come and pick them up. Even though it was against the rules, he asked her to come to the airport's drop-off point, since it was closer than the pick-up point.

Picture this: he is pushing two trolleys, one in each hand, each with 100 kg of luggage on them. Ami is still hysterical, pulling on his shirt, wanting to be carried. By this stage, Pete explained to me, he was at his limit. (Seriously, who wouldn't be?)

Now crying himself, Pete steps outside to the drop-off zone at Melbourne Airport – and immediately sees the security guy. This guy's job is to stop people like Pete stuffing up the system and getting picked up where they shouldn't. But he takes one look at Pete, sums up the situation, and grabs one of Pete's trolleys and pushes it to Trish's waiting car. Then he says, 'Good luck', and goes on his way.

People who work in service roles are often criticised for following the rules to the letter – not being flexible or adaptable – and I hear time and time again of employees who feel handcuffed by rules that destroy a great customer experience. However, this rules-based approach sometimes comes from frontline staff because they don't want to overburden their boss or are fearful of making a mistake.

This is the first barrier to creating a win-win solution with people we work with and serve. Service is about being human; it's about being in relationship. We must not let rules get in the way of that.

When it comes to relationships, rules are made to be bent or broken.

CUSTOMER SERVICE IN UNCERTAIN TIMES

In today's demanding world, taking a rigid approach to work and life will make things challenging for you. You need to be able to bend and flex to suit the situation. A major trauma like a global pandemic is the type of event that throughout human history has acted as a trigger to change human behaviour – and customer service, at its core, is an expression of human behaviour.

Millions of people have been devastated since the pandemic began, and the ripple effect is still to be fully realised. At the very least, mask-wearing, social distancing and unpredictable border closures that leave people in house arrest with little to no notice have gone from being unthinkable to being routine in day-to-day life.

What will customers expect from their local store attendant, cafe barista or petrol-station attendant? Ordinary experiences like buying groceries, grabbing a coffee and paying for petrol have been adapted so dramatically in the short term due to COVID-safe compliance that we are at risk of changing the way people behave forever.

A retail client of mine recently reviewed their operational procedures and discovered they hadn't been updated in ten years! A lot can happen in ten years. A lot has happened the past two years, two months and even two days. Vladimir Lenin said, 'There are decades where nothing happens and there are weeks where decades happen.'

Think about all the changes we are now adapting to, and how fast we are being asked to adapt. Policies, procedures and rules are usually put in place for good reasons; but then the workplace, business environment or customer needs change, and the rules don't change with them. Too often, we become unable to see what needs to be changed; we become cogs within a system, following processes even when they're out of date or irrelevant. We wait for our leaders to tell us what to do instead of seeing what needs to be done and doing that. Sometimes, we need to apply common sense.

COMMON SENSE

Remember, no matter how efficient you are at following rules, they can cloud your judgement about how to meet your customers' needs. Giving or expecting unquestioning compliance can, in fact, damage your relationships with customers, colleagues or staff.

If you have staff reporting to you, for example, and a new or unusual situation arises with a customer when you're not around, it's incredibly frustrating for the employee to feel that their hands are tied and they can't make a decision outside of the rules. No-one wins in this situation – and having staff heavily dependent on leaders to make decisions is a customer complaint waiting to happen. They need to be empowered to make good judgement calls and decisions in your absence.

If you're rigid and unable to be flexible when necessary to get the best outcomes, then you'll find it difficult to respond to an ever-changing world and take advantage of new opportunities.

Customers feel like they're a nuisance or aren't important when they're told 'it's our policy' or 'my supervisor won't let me do that', and managers usually hate having to enforce procedures and policies that make little sense. Sometimes the rules aren't challenged often enough or reassessed in light of real-life scenarios that are presenting themselves.

Rules exist to serve people, not enslave them.

Without rules, customer service would become chaotic, and employees and customers would never know what to expect. Remember, though: in service we are always trying to remove barriers for customers, and sometimes rules can put more unnecessary barriers in place.

READ THE CONTEXT AND ADAPT

Imagine shifting quickly from analysing a spreadsheet with your colleagues to responding to a distressed customer, or from serving an elderly lady who's hard of hearing to meeting a supplier and discussing product quality. Could you respond appropriately?

Shifting context throughout a day is one of the reasons why we feel so busy. Ideally, we'd be far more productive because we'd dedicate one entire day to analysing spreadsheets and then devote the next day to responding to distressed customers. We could get into the right mode for the day to suit the context, mentally prepare ourselves and find loads of flow in the day. Unfortunately, the reality is that it's just about impossible to stay in the same context all day. So, we have to be able to shift context and adapt in a way that appears effortless to the people we serve, picking up the next task or moving to the next interaction with focus and attention.

The trap, when we shift context, is that we may miss things. To be adaptable, you need context: you need to pay attention and 'read the room' so that you can reset and realign before you act or speak. When you miss context – say, that someone has shopped with you for 20 years, or that the supplier has delivered poor product three times this week – you're missing critical information for applying common sense and good judgement.

Then, if you're doing something and it's not working, or you're faced with a new scenario, you need to step back and ask:

Is there another way to approach this?

Service is, more often than not, situational. More than ever, we live in a world that is asking us to bend and flex a little. When we take a rigid approach without looking for alternatives or keeping an open mind, we may appear to be unable to adapt.

RED AND BLUE RULES

To be able to adapt easily, you need employees and leaders to have a conversation about what rules can be changed or bent. In any organisation, it's useful to recognise the difference between firm rules and assumptions or traditions. A useful shorthand for this is to divide rules into two types: red rules and blue rules.

Red rules

Red rules are rules that cannot be broken. They involve decisions that could be detrimental to the organisation, such as a safety procedure, or a legality issue such as serving alcohol to someone underage.

Blue rules

Blue rules are designed to make the service or operation run more smoothly. Blue rules apply to decisions that can't harm the organisation in any way – such as an operational procedure or a refund policy – meaning, they can be broken if necessary.

Identifying blue and red rules

Identifying the blue and red rules is one of the most empowering and proactive things a service team can do. By establishing what rules can be bent and giving people a framework for how to speak to the customer, they become more confident about dealing with 'grey area' issues in their leaders' absence. An additional benefit is that everyone is brought up to date on the current rules and procedures, and as a result, people start to think for themselves and come up with solutions for unlikely scenarios. Put a diverse group of people around a table and see how creative they can be with bendy rules!

I receive an email of thanks each week from a team leader or manager I have worked with telling me how empowering this conversation was for their team. Many organisations working in dynamic environments such as retail, real estate and airports tell me that blue and red rules should be reviewed quarterly as a minimum.

Let's not forget that the customer is also a winner. There's nothing more pleasing, as a customer who is faced with a situation that isn't straightforward, than when the person serving you is in a position to deal with it straight away. How great is that?

When you can't fulfil a customer's request involving a red rule:

1. Empathise with the customer: 'I understand why…'

2. Say no: '…but I can't do that.'

3. Explain the reason: 'Because we'd both be breaking the law.'

4. Let the customer know of anything you can do instead: 'But what I could do is…'

If you are bending blue rules, however, know your own limits in doing so. It never hurts to ask a manager or supervisor for their opinion if you are unsure. Equally, it's wise to have an understanding of why the rule is there in the first place and of any ripple effects or consequences that bending the rule will have.

If you fulfil a customer's request by bending a blue rule, I recommend that you follow these steps:

1. Empathise with the customer. For example, 'I understand why you feel…'

2. Explain the rule: 'Normally, I can't do that because…' (Sometimes this step isn't necessary, however: it depends on the situation, the customer and the rule.)

3. Explain that you can help: 'But I'll make a special exception for you.'

4. Remind them of the rule again: 'To make things easier in future…'

BEND BLUE RULES

Reflect now

- Where do you see an opportunity to be more adaptable in your role?
- When have you been more adaptable and seen an opportunity to make a change to a rule, or to bend the rule slightly? What was the outcome?
- Which rules do you know you can bend, and which do you know you cannot?

Embed the habit

A conversation about blue and red rules should be fun, and should include a diverse group of people so you get plenty of different ideas at the table. There will most certainly be disagreements about which rules are which, and that is great, because through the discussion you will realise why each rule is a rule in the first place. Here's a suggested process for discussing and agreeing on the blue and red rules in your business:

- Take a set of standard procedures and map them alongside customer scenarios.
- Nominate someone in the session to throw in a few curve balls to make each scenario more complex.
- Document the leaders' decision or agreement about when rules can be bent.
- List the blue rules up on a wall and the red rules beside them, and finalise them.

Revisit them often!

Service Habit 21
DO YOUR BEST

There's an old Chinese story I heard from my meditation teacher about a rice farmer who lived a very simple life. He had a small home, children and a rice field just big enough to feed and provide for his family. One day, a herd of wild horses came running through the village and ran into the farmer's field, where they got stuck in the mud and couldn't get away.

The man's neighbour came running over, saying, 'This is good news! Such good fortune! You're rich, this is amazing!' And the rice farmer said, 'Good news, bad news; who knows?' A few weeks later, his twelve-year-old son tried to ride one of the wild horses but got thrown off and broke his leg. The neighbour came running over and said, 'Oh no, this is such bad news!' And the farmer said, 'Good news, bad news; who knows?'

A week later, a general came marching through the village with his army to go to war, and enlisted every healthy boy more than ten years old. They didn't take the farmer's son, though, because he had a broken leg. The neighbour came running over: 'Yes! This is wonderful news, how lucky are you!' And the father replied, 'Good news, bad news; who knows?'

When I heard this story, I felt a great relief – it highlighted for me how quickly we label situations and draw conclusions that something is good or bad. We all have ups and downs in life – the good and the bad, the shadow and the light – and it's how you view things that matters. You need to have perspective and keep an open mind about what the whole picture might be.

It's the same in service environments. You're constantly presented with situations and experiences that could be labelled either good or bad, depending on how you look at them.

Service is not always easy, and we don't always get the outcome we were looking for. This final service habit is an invitation to remember to always do your best in each moment and focus on the process, not just the outcome.

GOOD VERSUS BAD

If I asked you right now to tell me all the good and bad things that happened to you today at work, I have no doubt you could. You've already decided whether these (very recent!) events were good or bad. For example:

- Today you lost a major account at work = bad news.
- Today you made your largest sale ever = good news.

The truth is, however, your judgements about what's catastrophic versus what's worth celebrating can be premature. For example:

- You might find out that the major account you lost is going into receivership and would have had no way of paying your bills = good news.
- That sale you just made, the largest ever? You might discover there's no stock left to fulfil it = bad news.

What if, rather than labelling something 'good' or 'bad', you labelled it, '*it just is*'.

By labelling something 'it just is', we are keeping an open mind about what may come next – and let's be honest, we never know what's coming next. What may appear good in this moment can turn out to be not so good in hindsight, and what appears bad in this moment can turn out to be the best thing that could have happened when we look back later.

Good news, bad news… do any of us really ever know?

WIN SOME, LOSE SOME

It's realistic to expect some speed bumps in service interactions, especially when dealing with humans, but don't let a 'lapse' become a 'collapse'. One failure is one failure: there's no need to catastrophise it.

The potential at work sometimes, when you are helping and serving others, is that you can get a bit too serious about it. When you take things too seriously, though – push too hard, cling to expected outcomes or experiences and try to control every situation – you may end up very disappointed and shrink away from your goal if things don't turn out the way you want. Consider the following:

· The last time you didn't meet a target at work, what was the inner dialogue you had?

· The last time you made a mistake or forgot some important information, how did you feel towards yourself, and how did that impact those around you?

· The last time you tried to do something different and it didn't work, or possibly even backfired, what was your mindset when you tried it again? Did you try again at all?

Your relationship to failure and setbacks is critical to your progress with the service habits, your service goals and your growth in life.

All you can ever do is your best in each moment. Let the outcome take care of itself.

> *In service, rather than asking, 'Was the outcome good or bad?' or 'Did I win or lose?' the question I want you to ask is, 'Did I do my best?'*

CONTROL THE CONTROLLABLES

I'm fairly certain that, for you to win in your job role, you rely on many people to do their bit well, too. Whether you're leading a team in a busy stadium, running a department, working out on site or in an office with a large team, you're responsible for your part of the service chain, and you rely on others to do their part to achieve overall customer success.

Working in a team is like playing a team sport. Everyone has a role to play out on the field, everyone knows the common goal and direction of the game, and everyone relies on the other team members being at the top of their game and playing to the best of their ability, so that together the whole team performs and ultimately wins. However, despite best intentions, the coach's training and guidance can't control the players and their performance. You can plan for things to go a certain way, but none of us really have any control over others – the only person you can control is yourself. You cannot control your teammates. You cannot control the customer.

In the first cluster of service habits in this book, under the pillar of 'Know yourself', we looked deeply at the things you can control: your reactions ('Take four seconds'), your thoughts ('Watch your thoughts') and your behaviours ('Be the change'). Great service starts with focusing on the parts you can control, and by staying in the present moment you will have the greatest influence on others. Outside of this, well – it's out of your control.

DOING YOUR BEST WITH STRENGTH AND SOFTNESS

If I stub my toe, I could become aware of the pain and yell at myself for being clumsy, but I wouldn't be exhibiting self-compassion or kindness. Alternatively, I could become aware of the pain and treat myself as if I were my best friend. I'd be gentle. I'd be kind. I'd be caring. I'd realise that it's only human to become distracted and stub your toe; we all do it from time to time.

If you hit a speed bump at work or in life, can you maintain focus with determination and strength, and balance that with kindness and compassion? We're continually told to be powerful, strong and steady in our approach to work, and these are wonderful qualities to have, but we also need to balance that with kindness.

When I was doing my yoga teacher training in 2013, one of the concepts I learned to help me teach students was the notion of *sthira* and *sukha*. In Sanskrit, *sthira* means 'strength' and *sukha* means 'softness': the idea is that you can bring both strength and softness to things – you can practise with strength in a relaxed manner. To sustain new service habits in your work life, it's important to notice times when you need to bring some *sukha* into a moment. For example:

- You can be laser-focused on your sales targets, yet allow the outcome to be what it will be.
- You can be firm in your expectations about a service team's output, yet be open and caring when a team member doesn't meet that expectation.

Most of us have plenty of sthira *but not enough* sukha. *Practise bringing softness into situations.*

PRACTISE SELF-COMPASSION

We are all becoming more conscious. That's what humans do; we evolve. A large part of being more conscious and evolving is bringing more compassion to ourselves.

Self-compassion means treating yourself with the same love and kindness that you would show a friend going through difficult times. Whether you have made mistakes, experienced failure or faced challenging circumstances, you are as deserving of your respect and warmth as anyone. After all, self-compassion is about being kind to yourself *because* you are a human being with human flaws.

Many mistakenly avoid self-compassion, believing that it means being easy on yourself and will lead to complacency. But self-compassion, in fact, is the foundation for resilience and helps you develop the courage to face hard facts. In taking a constructive – rather than critical or harsh – attitude toward your efforts as a professional, you build your capacity to navigate challenges and unpredictability.

By practising self-compassion, you can create a kind and caring place within you that is comforting and free of judgement – even in the toughest of times. Here are some of the benefits of self-compassion:

- You are able to handle any change or challenging situation with greater ease, calm and certainty – drawing from your inner resources, rather than waiting for the external world to change.

- The more you practise self-compassion, the more you can move from 'handling' to smooth sailing.

- Your relationships improve – the better you notice, understand and relate to your own internal experience, the more you can appreciate the experiences of others.

Ultimately, you can rise above setbacks and cope when it all goes to shit by activating self-compassion.

Self-compassion often takes a little more effort than compassion towards others, but it's one of the most effective ways to both motivate and care for yourself as a high performer in service. When I see someone practising self-compassion, I see them displaying empathy and taking action.

Kristin Neff teaches the Mindful Self-Compassion program, and defines self-compassion as having three main components:

1. self-kindness
2. a sense of common humanity
3. mindfulness.

'Self-kindness' means taking a warm and understanding approach towards yourself when you're suffering, have made a mistake or are feeling that you're not good enough. It's also about acknowledging when you're being critical and judgemental of yourself. If you find yourself in overwhelm throughout a working day, imagine you have a sticker on your clothing that says 'I'm practising self-kindness' as a trigger to be more kind and understanding towards yourself.

'A sense of common humanity' is about recognising that both suffering and personal inadequacy are part of the shared human experience. Often, it feels as if you are the only person failing or making mistakes, and you have an irrational feeling of isolation, but this isn't true. One of the best ways to feel a sense of common humanity is by sharing with others what you're experiencing or feeling: it's through sharing that we learn that others are also suffering. I encourage groups who are learning the service habits to dial into a group webinar once a month during the twelve-month implementation period, just to share and hear from each other about where they're winning and where they're suffering.

This not only strengthens the group culture but also strengthens self-compassion for individuals.

'Mindfulness' involves becoming aware of when you're suffering. It also means striving for a non-judgemental state of mind, in which you can observe your thoughts and feelings as they are without trying to suppress or deny them. When you see yourself identifying with a thought such as 'I'm a loser', or 'I'm hopeless at this task', it's a great practice to catch that thought and consider that your emotion towards yourself may be disproportionate. In this way, you gain some balance in that moment by observing your thoughts and emotions as a witness, without trying to suppress them or deny them – just seeing and slightly detaching from them.

Three steps to self-compassion

So, when you set a goal or a challenge – maybe you want to develop a habit, for example – and you fall flat or fail, how can you respond to yourself in a more compassionate way?

If you're 100 per cent committed to adopting the service habits and can see how they'll improve your relationships with yourself and those you serve, then here are three simple steps to becoming more self-compassionate when things don't work out the way you'd hoped:

1. *Acknowledge any setbacks.* This will enable you to release your grip on trying to get it right – it's the first step to self-compassion. After all, beating yourself up for not being able to do something won't change the situation, so save your energy and just acknowledge that it didn't work.

2. *Watch your self-talk.* Speak to yourself in a soothing tone, as if you were talking to a friend or child you care about, and tell yourself compassionately to honour and accept your humanness. Things won't always go the way you want them to. You don't have control over everything.

3. *Don't take yourself so seriously.* When you start practising these new service habits, can you approach them without attachment? Can you be light and playful with them?

Ideally, you would practise this self-compassion exercise on a daily basis, to slowly train your mind to incorporate self-compassion as a new habit.

Remember: everyone is doing the best they can at any moment in time, with the consciousness they have to work with – including you. Be kind and offer yourself the same empathy and compassion you'd extend to others.

Talk to yourself like you would to a friend.

DO YOUR BEST

Reflect now

- Think of a difficult situation at work currently. Have you labelled it 'good' or 'bad'?

- How much of your energy is focused on the things you cannot control?

- What are some self-critical dialogues that you've noticed you have had recently at work, and that you could relax and release?

- When you practise the service habits, who might you share your commitment with so they can gently remind you about them from time to time?

Embed the habit

- Over the coming week, commit to a conversation with a co-worker about the service habits and share the areas you're focusing on.

- Notice opportunities during that week to practise the three steps of self-compassion.

- A week later, circle back and share with your co-worker how you've gone. Seek feedback from them – have they noticed anything different in you? Most importantly, share your inner dialogue and self-talk during your practice of these habits. Are you talking to yourself like you would to a friend?

A word about bad habits

We've talked about 21 service habits that will help you give outstanding service – but before we finish, it's important we also talk briefly about habits you may need to let go of that may be working against you. These habits and behaviours usually make you feel safe and comfortable, but, in many ways, they prevent you from deepening relationships with those you serve. It's important you become conscious of them.

I call these habits collectively 'The Path of Obstacles', because they're like stones – and in some cases, boulders – that stop your colleagues or customers getting what they need. The habits may have been created with the right intention – for example, to achieve a guaranteed sale or a specific outcome – but you may not be aware of the cost and how these bad habits are impacting your working relationships.

The goal, to begin with, is just to notice whether you have any of these five habits:

1. trying to control the outcome
2. blaming others
3. gossiping
4. avoiding asking for help
5. complaining.

Let's look at each of these in turn.

TRYING TO CONTROL THE OUTCOME

As I've said before, humans are unpredictable creatures. So, when you serve people, you will not always know what response is coming your way. You can't control other people's reactions, and it's unrealistic to think that you're in complete control of a situation that involves another human being.

When you see yourself, at the beginning of an interaction with a colleague or customer, holding tightly onto the outcome you want or what you expect the other person to do or say, just remind yourself that you cannot control everything. Loosen your grip on your expectations. Service requires you to give up control of the outcome, and by doing so, you're honouring the other person and accepting what they bring to the situation.

BLAMING OTHERS

You know that saying, 'Don't throw your colleagues under the bus'? When there's been an error and people are under scrutiny, they sometimes like to inform others of the cause of the error – which can sometimes lead to blaming another member of the team in order to protect themselves.

None of us likes to be wrong, and when it comes to satisfying others, we genuinely always want the other person to feel that we've put our best foot forward to help them. So, when things go wrong or don't meet customers' or colleagues' standards, our ego is sometimes too quick to protect us by blaming someone else for the breakdown.

Service requires you to take full responsibility, especially when serving customers: you represent the brand, the business and the team, regardless of your role. When there's a breakdown in the service chain, it's better to direct your energy and effort towards creating a solution rather than pointing the finger at the person or people who caused the problem.

GOSSIPING

When I was 16 years old and working a shift at the local McDonald's one afternoon, I was assigned to take orders from the drive-through. I was the voice that came through the speaker, greeted people in their cars and took their orders. It was the early 1990s and our headsets were archaic and very manual: we had to push the top button to speak to the customer and the bottom button to speak to our colleague who was assembling the order.

On this day, I was greeted by a customer who was screaming into the speaker box rudely. After tolerating a disjointed conversation with her, I asked her to come around to the window to complete the order. Then, instead of pushing the bottom button to speak to my colleague and comment about the customer's choice of language, I accidentally pressed the top button. The customer heard my judgemental, childish comments and sped around the drive-through demanding to speak to a manager.

The lesson was learned at a very young age: never gossip about anyone, ever. It's an energy-waster and it never does any good. If you're ever tempted to gossip about a customer, stop and think about my story before you do. Ask yourself, 'What will gossiping about this person achieve? Is there something more productive I could do, like getting on with providing them with a solution?'

AVOIDING ASKING FOR HELP

In a service environment, you're continually presented with situations that may never have occurred before, let alone been planned for. Sometimes, people hold off asking for help in such situations because they're afraid of looking silly or not having all the answers. This is a limiting belief.

Chances are, you're part of a team and you play a significant role in helping others get their jobs done. This means you also play a significant role in serving the customer, solving problems and removing barriers for them. In order for you and the people around you to perform at your best professional level, you must put the person you're serving at the centre of the situation. If you're refraining from asking for help, you're putting yourself at the centre. You're allowing your pride and ego to be more dominant than the needs of the individual you're serving.

There's nothing wrong with asking for help. The best professionals in service are those who are confident enough to know their strengths and humble enough to know their limitations – which means that from time to time, they ask for help.

COMPLAINING

In his book *How to Win Friends and Influence People*, Dale Carnegie states, 'Any fool can criticize, condemn, and complain – and most fools do. But it takes character and self-control to be understanding and forgiving.'

Repeated complaining over time wires your brain for more future complaining. It becomes a habit, and you soon find it easier to be negative than positive.

Business environments are dynamic, unpredictable and sometimes a little messy. No customer-facing team needs a member looking for negativity: there's already enough to work through as it is! If you're interviewing someone for a service role and in the small talk they complain about the weather, the airline they travel with or their internet connectivity, it's usually a bad sign.

If you notice something that needs attention or improvement, the best way to serve yourself, your team and your customer is to raise it in a solutions-focused way. Stick to the facts, which are always neutral.

FORGE A NEW PATH

In her book *A Return to Love*, Marianne Williamson reminds us that we all have the same opportunity in every encounter to give to others and serve humanity. That includes casual encounters, such as a customer you meet once, as well as encounters that are part of sustained relationships, such as with a long-term colleague or employee.

You will always have something to learn from the people you serve, regardless of the power you or they hold. When you are in service to others, they will teach you something about yourself that will make you a better person – that's just one of the universal laws in life.

So, think about whether you have any of these bad service habits and, if so, how they may be impeding you when you serve people. To let go of something, first you have to be aware of it. Once you're aware you have a bad service habit and decide that you want to let go of it, you make more room for the good service habits you've learned about in this book.

Remember what Gandhi said: 'The best way to find yourself is to lose yourself in the service of others.'

You've got this

Your impact on others matters. It matters to you, and it matters to those you serve. If you choose to adopt these service habits, you can transform your approach to service and expand into your best professional self. When you're serving people, even in the simplest interaction, you can move them in a positive direction and elevate even the most ordinary moments in a day.

I believe in you and your commitment to transform relationships. If you have read this book up until this page, you are eager to wake up and serve in a more conscious way, every day. You're open to growth and to expanding yourself. You're eager to improve relationships, which will improve the quality of your life, personally and professionally. In fact, the feedback I get from many of my clients is that people apply the service habits at home as well as at work.

So, practise the habits like you've always been doing them – treat this book as a reminder of something you already know how to do. Don't doubt, don't hesitate; be all in, 100 per cent. If you forget, the answers are in this book. If you lose this book, the answers are within you. I'm your biggest supporter when it comes to deepening your relationships with those you serve, and you'll always find me on the sidelines cheering you on. (You can email me directly at hello@serviceq.co.)

At the end of the day, ask yourself: 'Could I have made a greater impact on those I served today?'

Make sure the answer is always 'No', and that you know in your heart that you've been the brightest version of yourself in each and every ordinary moment.

The journey is worth it. The change you see in yourself and the reactions from others will be truly priceless! I'm a better person for stepping into serving people more consciously and intentionally, and with more heart – and habits have been the formula for achieving this.

My wish for you is that you love being in service like you never did before. My wish is that the relationships you form at work and with your customers deepen and strengthen effortlessly. My wish is that you find each habit easy to follow and can use the exercises and activities to start making change immediately.

I look forward to hearing your story about the changes you've made and the reactions from those around you. Write to me at hello@serviceq.co!

Jaquie

Resources

Here are the resources I've mentioned in the book, in case you'd like to dig further into the various topics.

Introduction

B.J. Fogg, *Tiny Habits: The small changes that change everything*, Penguin Books Australia, Melbourne, 2019.

James Clear, *Atomic Habits: An easy and proven way to build good habits and break bad ones*, Random House Business Books, London, 2018.

Robin Sharma, 'How heroes install habits', *The Personal Mastery Recordings*, video recording, robinsharma.com.

1. Choose to serve

Kahlil Gibran, 'On work', in *The Prophet*, Alfred A. Knopf, 1923.

2. Create helpful beliefs

Chris Helder, *Useful Belief: Because it's better than positive thinking*, John Wiley, Milton, Queensland, 2016.

3. Take four seconds

Max Strom, *A Life Worth Breathing*, Skyhorse Publishing, New York, 2010.

Peter Bregman, *Four Seconds: All the time you need to stop counter-productive habits and get the results you want*, HarperCollins Publishers Inc, New York, 2016.

4. Watch your thoughts

Erin Winick, 'With brain-scanning hats, China signals it has no interest in workers' privacy', Future of Work column, *MIT Technology Review*, technologyreview.com, 30 April 2018.

5. Meditate daily

Rasmus Hougaard & Jacqueline Carter, 'How to practice mindfulness throughout your work day', *Harvard Business Review*, hbr.org, 4 March 2016.

Jon Kabat-Zinn, *Wherever You Go, There You Are: Mindfulness meditation in everyday life*, Hyperion, New York, 1994.

Christina Congleton, Britta K. Hölzel & Sara W. Lazar, 'Mindfulness can literally change your brain', *Harvard Business Review*, hbr.org, 8 January 2015.

Gaëlle Desbordes, Lobsang T. Negi, Thaddeus W.W. Pace, B. Alan Wallace, Charles L. Raison and Eric L. Schwartz, 'Effects of mindful-attention and compassion meditation training on amygdala response to emotional stimuli in an ordinary, non-meditative state', *Frontiers in Human Neuroscience*, 1 November 2012, https://doi.org/10.3389/fnhum.2012.00292.

Jillian Lavender, 'Is meditation the science-backed way to slow down the ageing process?', *Getthegloss.com*, 12 February 2018.

6. Be the change

American Express, September 2013 Service Study, trendwatching.com/trends/future-customer-service.

Michael Henderson, *Above the Line: How to create a company culture that engages employees, delights customers and delivers results*, John Wiley, Milton, Queensland, 2014.

Dr Wayne W. Dyer, *Everyday Wisdom for Success*, Hay House, Inc., Carlsbad, California, 2006.

7. Look the part

Mark Schaller, 'Evolutionary bases of first impressions', in Nalini Ambady & John J. Skowronski (eds), *First Impressions*, Guilford Press, New York, 2008.

Rob Nelissen & Marijn Meijers, 'Social benefits of luxury brands as costly signals of wealth and status', *Evolution and Human Behaviour*, vol. 32, no. 5, September 2011, pp. 343–355.

Albert E. Mannes, 'Shorn scalps and perceptions of male dominance', *Social Psychological and Personality Science*, vol. 4, no. 2, March 2013, pp. 198–205.

Randy J. Larsen & Todd K. Shackelford, 'Gaze avoidance: Personality and social judgments of people who avoid direct face-to-face contact', *Personality and Individual Differences*, vol. 21, no. 6, December 1996, pp. 907–917.

Mark Stibich, 'Top 10 reasons to smile every day', Verywellmind, 2 April 2021, www.verywellmind.com/top-reasons-to-smile-every-day-2223755.

Amy Cuddy, *Presence: Bringing your boldest self to your biggest challenges*, The Orion Publishing Group, London, 2015.

8. Put the team first

Michael Liley, Patricia Feliciano & Alex Laurs, *Employee Experience Reimagined*, Accenture, accenture.com, 2017.

9. Use their name

Dale Carnegie, *How to Win Friends and Influence People*, Harper Collins Publishers (Australia) Pty Ltd, Sydney, 2017.

10. See their world

Daniel Goleman, *Emotional Intelligence: Why it can matter more than IQ*, Random House USA, Inc., New York, 2005.

Daniel Goleman, 'Social intelligence and the biology of leadership', *Harvard Business Review*, September issue, 2008.

Thich Nhat Hanh, *How to Love*, Ebury Publishing, London, 2016.

11. Listen to understand

Nathalie Fernbach & Sally Rafferty, 'Townsville Hospital hosts humanoid robot in Australian first trial', *ABC News*, abc.net.au, 24 August 2018.

Daniel H. Pink, *To Sell is Human*, Riverhead Books, New York, 2012.

Amy Cuddy, *Presence: Bringing your boldest self to your biggest challenges*, The Orion Publishing Group, London, 2015.

12. Squint with your ears

Dilip Bhattacharjee, Jesus Moreno & Francisco Ortega, 'The secret to delighting customers: putting employees first', McKinsey & Company, mckinsey.com, March 2016.

Judith E. Glaser, *Conversational Intelligence: How great leaders build trust and get extraordinary results*, Routledge, London, 2016.

13. Test your assumptions

Malcolm Gladwell, *Blink: The power of thinking without thinking*, Penguin Books Ltd, UK, 2006.

Matthias J. Gruber, Bernard D. Gelman & Charan Ranganathstudy, 'States of curiosity modulate hippocampus-dependent learning via the dopaminergic circuit', *Neuron*, vol. 84, no. 2, 22 October 2014, pp. 486–496.

14. Ask better questions

Dale Carnegie, *How to Win Friends and Influence People*, Harper Collins Publishers (Australia) Pty Ltd, Sydney, 2017.

Alison Wood Brooks and Leslie K. John, 'The surprising power of questions', *Harvard Business Review*, hbr.org, May–June 2018.

16. Praise effectively

Courtney E. Ackerman, 'What is positive psychology & why is it important?', *Positivepsychology.com*, 6 December 2020, https://positivepsychology.com/what-is-positive-psychology-definition.

Shawn Achor, 'The benefits of peer-to-peer praise at work', *Harvard Business Review*, hbr.org, 19 February 2016.

17. Tell the truth

University of Chicago Booth School of Business, 'People can handle the truth (more than you think)', *ScienceDaily*, 19 September 2018, www.sciencedaily.com/releases/2018/09/180919133003.htm.

Dale Carnegie, *How to Win Friends and Influence People*, Harper Collins Publishers (Australia) Pty Ltd, Sydney, 2017.

18. Look after your Shakti

TSheets by QuickBooks, 'Lunch: an endangered privilege in Australia', tsheets.com.au, 2017.

Daniel H. Pink, *When: The scientific secrets of perfect timing*, Text Publishing, Melbourne, 2018.

Donna McGeorge, *The First 2 Hours: Make better use of your most valuable time*, John Wiley, Milton, Queensland, 2019.

The Tim Ferriss Show podcast, 'LeBron James and his top-secret trainer, Mike Mancias (#349)', 27 November 2018, https://tim.blog/2018/11/27/lebron-james-mike-mancias.

Scott Davis, 'LeBron James reportedly spends $1.5 million per year to take care of his body — here's where it goes', *Business Insider Australia*, 14 July 2018, www.businessinsider.com.au/how-lebron-james-spends-money-body-care-2018.

19. Minimise multitasking

Edward M. Hallowell, *CrazyBusy: Overstretched, overbooked, and about to snap! Strategies for handling your fast-paced life*, Ballantine Books, New York, 2007.

Paul Atchley, 'You can't multitask, so stop trying', *Harvard Business Review*, hbr.org, 21 December 2010.

A word about bad habits

Dale Carnegie, *How to Win Friends and Influence People*, Harper Collins Publishers (Australia) Pty Ltd, Sydney, 2017.

Marianne Williamson, *A Return to Love: Reflections on the principles of A Course in Miracles*, HarperCollins Publishers, 1997.

Acknowledgements

One of the simplest ways to serve people is to first acknowledge them. Acknowledging people when they give you their time, their attention, their knowledge and their love is such an easy, humane thing to do, and it's a practice I try to live each day as the moment presents itself. When I am extraordinarily present, the moment always has something to offer me, to teach me, to allow me to experience. I have a whole lifetime of acknowledgements to capture up until now, and I would like to think that I have expressed gratitude and love privately to those in my life who help shape me and my work every single day. With the little space allowed to me here, I'd like to thank everybody who has made this book possible: my partner, Costa, first and foremost, whose undeniable love for people and life makes him a living, walking example of what it takes to deepen relationships. He's always encouraging me to follow what makes my heart sing and providing me with exceptional perspectives to help me further shape my points of view. My father has been a stunning role model in my lifetime of discipline, service and curiosity. He also kept me abreast of current affairs and worldly news when my head was down and I was only focused on writing the book and nothing else. My closest and dearest friend Taryn Pieramati has helped facilitate many Service Habits workshops over the years, providing me with interesting insights and perspectives and an abundance of love and support during a phase of growth and intense creativity. My editor Vanessa Smith, who made the approach to this second edition effortless and enjoyable, and to

Kelly Irving, my editor for the first edition who has supported my writing ideas over the years.

Lesley Williams and the team at Major Street Publishing, thank you again for believing in me as you did for the first book, and for all your care and hard work in the final production of this book – I just love working with you guys. Yianni, my designer and member of my family, who has pushed my brand and design elements this year to a new level and supports me in all my crazy dreams and ventures. Finally, to my mentor and dear friend Peter Cook, who inspired me to write the second edition, who did the belief for me at times when I could not and gave me a framework to ensure that this book, like so many other world-class books, is simple, elegant, useful and profound. I hope that I have achieved this with the words and stories that have been so carefully considered in this second edition.

ServiceQ Programs

Jaquie Scammell is the founder of ServiceQ, a business that exists to create training programs and experiences to help organisations achieve their potential through conscious leaders, engaged employees and loyal customers.

With a variety of programs for all sizes and sectors, world-class facilitators and a combination of online and face-to-face training experiences, ServiceQ has the perfect pathway to fit you and your team in achieving service transformation.

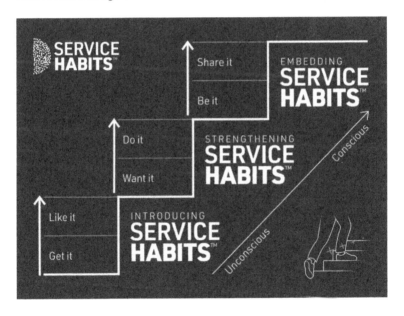

For information about the various Service Habits pathways, go to **serviceq.co/programs**.

Also by Jaquie Scammell

If you're looking to transform the customer service culture in your organisation, to decrease complaints and increase compliments, Jaquie Scammell's approach is simple and more human than simply introducing better processes and procedures – and her approach works.

Jaquie has studied Australian organisations that provide the best customer service and from this research she has created a system which, if followed, will increase loyalty to your business. You too will be able to create a winning customer service mindset that will be adopted by your frontline service leaders, the people who impact your customer service staff, who impact your customers every day.

'I recommend this book... to any leader wanting to build an exciting and dynamic organisation founded on great customer service.'

DAVID THODEY, AO

majorstreet.com.au

major st
PUBLISHING

We hope you enjoy reading this book. We'd love you to post a review on social media or your favourite bookseller site. Please include the hashtag #majorstreetpublishing.

Major Street Publishing specialises in business, leadership, personal finance and motivational non-fiction books. If you'd like to receive regular updates about new Major Street books, email info@majorstreet.com.au and ask to be added to our mailing list.

Visit majorstreet.com.au to find out more about our books (print, audio and ebooks) and authors, read reviews and find links to our Your Next Read podcast.

We'd love you to follow us on social media.

- linkedin.com/company/major-street-publishing
- facebook.com/MajorStreetPublishing
- instagram.com/majorstreetpublishing
- @MajorStreetPub